LIBRARY SERVICES
Challenges and Solutions in Digital Era

LIBRARY SERVICES

Challenges and Solutions in Digital Era

Edited by
Mrs Sandhya Aggarwal
Librarian, Manohar Memorial P.G. College, Fatehabad (Haryana)
Foreword by
Dr R. D. Mehla
Librarian, Kurukshetra University, Kurukshetra

Ess Ess Publications
New Delhi
in association with
MANOHAR MEMORIAL P.G. COLLEGE, FATEHABAD

Library Services

Challenges & Solutions in Digital Era

ISBN: 978-81-7000-658-9

Rs.575/-

First Published 2012

Published by:
Ess Ess Publications
4837/24, Ansari Road,
Darya Ganj,
New Delhi-110 002.
INDIA
Phones: 23260807, 41563444
Fax: 41563334
E-mail: info@essessreference.com
www.essessreference.com

Cover Design by *Patch Creative Unit*

Printed and bound in India at Salasar Imaging Systems.

Contents

Preface

A Library has aptly been defined as a Heaven for studious persons where we confront the thoughts of different scholars and writers, authors and critics on vast multitudes of disciplines under the sun.

The aim of this publication is to present the concept of 'Library Services with Technology' in its contemporary perspective and try to sensitize the librarians, teachers, scholars, information seekers and students etc. to the state-of-the-art modes of access and services in the field of Library Science.

I wish to profusely and gratefully thank all the scholars, librarians of different universities and colleges, experts and scientists in Library and Information Sciences who have contributed their highly informative and insightful articles for the book. I am equally indebted to the teaching and administrative staffs of my Institution who were greatly instrumental in making this endeavour a grand success. I express my deep and reverent gratitude to our worthy and dynamic Director of M. M. Group of Institutions Prof. Subhash Sharma and the Principal Dr. D. K. Kaushik who guided me and stood by me at every step.

My thanks are no less due to Ess Ess Publication, New Delhi who made the publication of the book possible in such a short time. I shall feel amply rewarded if this book renders any help to those concerned with Library as an Institution.

(Ms) Sandhya Aggarwal
Librarian,
Manohar Memorial P.G. College, Fatehabad

Foreword

In the 21st Century the role of the library and the librarian is going to be entirely changed because of ICT applications. The libraries play a vital role in the information world by providing access to world-class information resources and services and can help to stimulate research by promoting collection and services widely.

In future, no doubt, the environment of the libraries and information centres will be changed drastically but traditional skills and roles of the libraries and the librarian will still be needed. The basic role of a librarian is to evaluate and provide the information. The knowledge resources will, however, not change. It is assumed that in the emerging Internet & Website culture, every one can do searches but the reality is that it will become more difficult in future. Firstly, the developments are emerging fast as well as multi-dimensional and users are very busy. Secondly, most of them have no idea how search engines work and also lack expertise about the quality for integrity of the information they access.

In future the shape of the library will be changed into cyber library where the library services will be managed by electronic gadgets, robots and machines effectively. So library professionals need to be fully techno-savvy. Technology should, however, not become the master, it should rather serve as a servant.

R.D. Mehla

Librarian, Kurukshetra University, Kurukshetra

1

Information Literacy: The Lifeline of Lifelong Learning

Dr. Jagtar Singh
Professor and Head
Department of Library and Information Science,
Punjabi University, Patiala (Punjab) INDIA

ABSTRACT

This paper is based on the assumption that information and education have a critical role to play in socio-economic development and human progress. It emphasizes the need for promoting the concept and practice of information literacy across frontiers in the context of emerging knowledge economy. It underlines that the value of knowledge and information lies in their use, hence every effort must be made to put knowledge to work. Information literacy is the best way to promote the use of knowledge and information across frontiers. The paper takes cognizanse of the paradigm shift in libraries, and focuses on Seven Faces of Information Literacy and Six Frames of Information Literacy Education, 'Empowering 8 Model of Information Literacy' and Information Literacy Standards.

It refers to the United Nations' Millennium Development Goals (MDGs), UNESCO's Education for All Programme (EFAP), and Information for All Programme (IFAP), as well as the mandate of the National Knowledge Commission (NKC). It also highlights the impact of ICT on the life and work of people, and paradigm shift in libraries. It emphasizes that library consortia, institutional repositories, and open access archives are strategic response to the paradoxical situation of growing digital documents and declining library budgets. It also highlights the challenges and opportunities facing libraries, and concludes that though the future of libraries is uncertain, yet it is in the hands of the committed and competent library and information professionals.

Keywords : Information Literacy, Lifelong Learning, Seven Faces of Information Literacy, Six Frames of Information Literacy Education, Empowering 8 Model of Information Literacy, Information Literacy Standards

INTERNATIONAL AND NATIONAL INITIATIVES

Learning liberates and knowledge eliminates ignorance and ensures human progress. In fact, it is a well know fact that education liberates people from darkness and empowers them with knowledge, competencies, skills and attitudes to become assets for human progress across frontiers. That is why every nation puts premium on education to take its people to next level of consciousness. Taking cognizance of this fact, United Nations (UN) has set up the following seven Millennium Development Goals to be achieved by the year 2015.

Goal 1: Eradicate extreme poverty and hunger

Goal 2: Achieve universal primary education

Goal 3: Promote gender equality and empower women

Goal 4: Reduce child mortality

Goal 5: Improve maternal health

Goal 6: Combat HIV/AIDS, malaria and other diseases, and

Goal 7: Ensure environmental sustainability

UNESCO also has two ambitious programmes namely, Education for All Programme (EDAP) and Information for All Programme (IFAP) to spread education among member nations, and provide timely access to information to one and all in a cost-effective manner. Education, information literacy, and capacity building are the thrust areas for the UNESCO. In India, the Prime Minister has constituted a National Knowledge Commission (NKC) in the year 2005 under the Chairmanship of Mr. Sam Pitroda who brought telecommunication revolution in India. The NKC is focusing on expansion and excellence of higher education, and inclusion of left out categories in the field of higher education. The National Knowledge Commission is concerned with the following five key areas:

Access to knowledge; Knowledge concepts; Creation of knowledge; Knowledge applications, and Delivery of services

India is the first country in the world to establish a National Knowledge Commission (NKC) with a view:

1. To build excellence in the education system to meet the knowledge challenges of the 21st century and increase India's competitive advantage in fields of knowledge;
2. To promote creation of knowledge in science and technology institutions and laboratories;
3. To improve the management of institutions working on intellectual property rights;
4. To promote knowledge applications in agriculture and industry; and
5. To promote the use of knowledge capabilities in making government an effective, transparent and accountable

service provider to the citizens, and promote wide spread sharing of knowledge to maximize public benefit.

In its recommendations submitted to the Prime Minister of India, the NKC has recommended the opening of 1500 more universities by the year 2015 to enhance Gross Enrolment Ratio (GER) to 15%, and set up a National Commission on Libraries to provide massive access to quality information in a cost effective manner. The education budget has been increased three fold, and Rs. 10, 000 million have been promised to improve the library and information infrastructure in India. These recommendations and promises will certainly go a long way to improve the quality of life and work of people all across India.

PARADIGM SHIFT

Information and communication technology (ICT) has made a deep impact on all types of libraries. Today the elite are immensly benefited the power of digital and virtual libraries. At the same time we are very much worried about the future of libraries and the info-poor. The future of libraries is dependent both on external and internal changes. The ICT is providing the library and information professionals (LIPs) with both opportunities and challenges. There is a paradigm shift from standalone libraries to library and information networks; from printed publications to digital documents; and from ownership to access. This transition is the result of the impact of ICTs, the Internet and the web on different types of libraries. If we look around, many educational, social, economic, cultural, political, and technological changes are taking place. In the context of libraries and information centers (LICs), economic and technological changes have made a profound impact. Economically speaking, LICs are faced with a diametrically opposite situation with growing electronic resources and services on the one hand, and declining library budgets and library use on the other. There is a tremendous pressure on the library and informational professionals (LIPs) to justify the need for their existence in view of the fact that the library users are moving away from the libraries. It is high time to ascertain that why this is happening and what is the way out to bring back the users to the fold of libraries. Perhaps we have failed to come up to the expectations of the end users. It is high time to sensitize the information seekers about the value of library resources and services in achieving their educational, professionals, social and personal goals. They must be equipped with media and information literacy skills. As defined by Association of College and Research Libraries (ACRL) information literacy encompasses the following set of skills:

1. Knowing when information is needed
2. Finding information efficiently
3. Evaluating its quality
4. Using it effectively for a purpose, and
5. Observing ethical use of information

Basically, the future of libraries is in the hands of library users. Unfortunately, the end-users have fallen in the hands of commercial database providers and search engines like Google. The Net Generation thinks that Google has answer to all their queries. That is not true, and at stake is the quality of information and future of libraries. There is an immediate need to turn the rote learners into independent learners and critical thinkers. The challenge for today's teachers, including librarians, is to effectively educate students on how to strategically gather information from the Internet and other sources in ways that yield the best sources in a minimal amount of time. To develop into professional information managers, students must learn information skills for effective searching. Students need to move beyond their academic assignments for being able to complete research for their work. If universities are to prepare graduates to be excellent professionals, then we must place information literacy skills at the core of instruction in every discipline. This can best be accomplished when librarians in collaboration with classroom faculty infuse information literacy instruction into and across the curriculum. For this students and faculty need to be motivated to work in collaboration with library professionals to integrate information literacy (IL) across frontiers. Information literacy is the only way to enable people to make efficient, effective, creative, legal, ethical and strategic use of information for achieving their goals.

STRATEGIC PROFESSIONAL RESPONSE

The organization culture, library leadership and trained library personnel play a pivotal role in determining the role and status of libraries. LIPs are faced with a diametrically opposite situation with growing electronic resources on the one hand, and declining library budgets on the other. This has led to a paradoxical situation of paucity in plenty. There is a lot of unreliable information on the web in the public domain. LIPs are required to learn the art of finding needle from the hay stack. It is a profound challenge as the haystack is growing and the needle is moving from time to time. Information literacy is the way out to manage chaos on the web and ensure end-user satisfaction. Shared subscription, library consortia, institutional repositories, and open access archives are the outcome of our strategic response to deal with the challenge of declining library budgets. Instead of worrying about the future of libraries, we must learn to do the gap analysis and the SWOT analysis. We are required to ask a question from ourselves. The question is "Why the end-user is going to the Google by leaving behind the library?" Perhaps we have failed to come up to the expectations of the end users.

The effectiveness of library service lies at the point where the horizontal and vertical lines cross each other. In other words, where there is the perfect matching of end users' information needs, and library and information professionals' competence to meet those needs. Are we doing that? We must put this question to ourselves, and we will get a perfect answer to our worries about the future of libraries. For bright future, the LIPs must identify with the end-users. It is our experience after conducting many workshops in India and Bangladesh that the information seekers either are not aware of the availability of information resources and services, or do not have the appropriate skills to make use of those facilities. Even then the library and Informational Professionals (LIPs) are not sitting silently with their fingers crossed. Library consortia, institutional repositories, knowledge repositories, open source software, and open source gateways are the strategic responses being adopted by the LIPs across the globe to provide instant access to pertinent information to stakeholders in a cost-effective and timely manner. And they are fairly successful.

INFORMATION SKILLS FOR LEARNING

For making use of analog and digital resources and services, information seekers and library users are required to develop certain habits and attitudes along with acquiring a set of information skills for learning. Information Literacy encompasses all these skills. It includes basic, computer, media, network and cultural literacy. It facilitates learning and learning is not a destination in itself rather it is a lifelong process or a journey towards human progress. According to

UNESCO Report, *"Learning: The Resource Within"*, there are four pillars of learning and these are:

1. Learning to know
2. Learning to do
3. Learning to be, and
4. Learning to live together

Learning to know means that the stakeholders must have sound knowledge of philosophical and theoretical foundations of the subject; learning to do means active learning or learning by doing which includes hands-on-experience; whereas learning to be means learning to be a face in the crowd or being a competent person with complete mastery of one's domain; and finally learning to live together means developing a shared vision and internalizing a spirit of team learning. In fact, real learning cannot take place unless students value the learning they receive. Thus, universities must change students' attitudes toward the Internet. Faced with a generation of learners who believe books are an obsolete tool of learning and that libraries are merely book repositories, librarians and faculty must persuade young researchers to recognize the perils of using the Internet without a filter of critical thinking to determine the reliability and validity of the information they gather from the World Wide Web. Basically, books provide us the comfort of companionship and luxury of solitude. Unlike TV and the Internet, books and radio are a hot medium as they fire our imagination. Just as dirty water can cause many diseases; similarly unreliable information can lead to wrong decisions. In fact, quality of decisions depends on quality of information available to the stakeholders. Information literacy is another name of the ability for independent learning and critical thinking

CHALLENGES AND OPPORTUNITIES

With the ascent of digital documents and digital libraries, library and information professionals' role has expanded and challenges increased many fold. These challenges relate to capacity building, collection management, knowledge organization, digital preservation, online searching, content management, knowledge management, and promoting the use of libraries and networks. LIPs are required to work as leaders, managers, and facilitators. The ICT and the Internet has thrown open the doors to the LIPs to many opportunities. Now 24x7x365 access to information is available and the library is becoming a private place instead of a public space. LIPs have the opportunity to provide global reach to the indigenous knowledge. Similarly, we can get access to world's knowledge and information through the Internet, provided we have the will, skill, and the appropriate attitude. These opportunities and challenges can be handled effectively only by competent library personnel. Sound knowledge base, pertinent skills and pro-active, positive and open mind-set are essential components of a competent library and information professional. Do we have these attributes? If not, then the future of libraries is certainly uncertain. If yes, then there is no reason to worry about the future of libraries. LIPs must go out of the way to promote the concept and practice of information literacy. IL is only the expansion of our professional philosophy. Earlier we were talking of library instruction, bibliographic instruction and user education. Today we talk of IL.

CHANGE MANAGEMENT

According to Peter Senge, following five factors can go a long way to enable people to manage change and stay ahead of time:

1. Systems thinking
2. Shared vision
3. Positive and open mindset
4. Personal mastery, and
5. Team learning

It's a well known fact that value of knowledge and information lies in use. Hence most important challenge today is to create awareness of knowledge resources with particular focus on digital resources and services. Information literacy can serve as a critical tool to facilitate learning that is a lifelong process. Learning is not an end in itself; rather it is a journey towards socio-economic development and human progress. Information literacy is the tool to enable the end-users to become independent learners and critical thinkers. But unfortunately the concept of and practice of information literacy, as well as the spirit of service has not gained ground to the desirable level across frontiers. We are trying to process the multidimensional universe of knowledge and information with unidirectional mind-set. The technology is developing at the rocket speed and our mind-sets are moving at mule's speed. We are trying to process the 24x7 phenomenon with a 9x5 mind-set. That is the root cause of many of our problems.

INFORMATION CONSOLIDATION AND REPACKAGING

Like other stakeholders across frontiers, library and information professionals are also under tremendous pressure to manage change in libraries and information centres. There are both external and internal pressures. Externally, the ICT, the Internet, the Google, and the commercial information providers are giving fierce competition to libraries and library personnel. Internally, organizational culture, declining library budgets, and lethargic and apathetic attitude of majority of LIPs to change are the critical factors for the present state of the art. The end result is that the end-users are moving away from libraries and getting carried away by the commercial publishers and search engine like Google. It is high time that LIPs adopt a pro-active attitude, internalize team spirit, develop professional and personal competencies, and learn to be a face in the crowd of information providers. Librarians are the best professionals to organize knowledge and information to save the time of the information seekers. There is a lot of chaos in the public domain on the web. Librarians are required to retrieve pertinent information from the web, consolidate and repackage it for the benefit of the end-users. In the digital age, customization and personalization of information is the heart of the matter. LIPs can do that in a professional way by using the best professional practices, such as library classification, library cataloguing, concept indexing, bibliographical control and vocabulary control. But for doing that LIPs must be on sound footing with regard to the philosophy of library and information science, its theoretical foundations and best practices. Information literacy is the best way to sensitize the college students about the value of library resources and services in achieving their personal and educational goals.

LEADERSHIP AND COLLABORATION

There is great difference between a leader and a manager, as well as competence and competencies. A leader facilitates change but a manager maintains the status quo. Similarly, competence means complete mastery and competencies means a set of skills. These can be hard as well as soft skills. Competence comes with experience. However, before that we must have commonsense and formal education. Then the LIPs must internalize strategic professional learning as a lifelong learning process. LIPs must be equipped with cultural literacy and information skills for learning for creating the ripple effect among the faculty and students. Similarly, a sense of responsibility and accountability along with team spirit, motivation and interpersonal skills should also become a part of their mind, body, and soul. Only that way, the LIPs can make sense of the web-based chaos. Here T.S. Elliot reminds one of the lines:

Where is the wisdom?

We have lost in knowledge.

Where is the knowledge?

We have lost in information.

LIPs must learn to identify the domains of data, information, knowledge, and wisdom. Data are stray facts in context, information is meaningful data, which eliminates uncertainty and facilitates decision-making. Knowledge helps in problem solving, and wisdom warns us about the consequences of our decisions and actions. Library leaders are also required to promote the use of knowledge and information. Information seekers are having more and more of everything but less and less of time. Ranganathan advises LIPs to save the time of the readers. Personalization is the only way out as information needs of end users are highly personal. These needs vary from person to person, place to place and time to time. A reader requesting a dictionary is not interested in the whole dictionary; rather he is interested in the meaning of a particular word. In addition, he needs be trained in the skills of using various sources of information and the media associated with information. While designing information literacy programmes the focus must be on the perceptions of the information seekers. In this context, Seven Faces of Information Literacy provide useful input.

SEVEN FACES OF INFORMATION LITERACY

Christine Bruce has conducted research on information seekers' perceptions of information literacy and she has identified seven faces of information literacy. These are:

1. The information technology conception. Information literacy is seen as using information technology for information retrieval and communication.
2. The information sources conception. Information literacy is seen as finding information located in information sources.
3. Information process conception. Information literacy is seen as executing a process.
4. The information control conception. Information literacy is seen as controlling information.
5. The knowledge construction conception. Information literacy is seen as building up a personal knowledge base in a new area of interest.
6. The knowledge extension conception. Information literacy is seen as working with knowledge and personal perspectives adopted in such a way that novel insights are gained.
7. The wisdom conception. Information literacy is seen as using information wisely for the benefit of others.

But, basically, information literacy includes all these faces and should not be seen as individual facets. Similarly, you see in the next section that Susie Andretta has also given reflections on six frames of information literacy.

SIX FRAMES OF INFORMATION LITERACY EDUCATION

According to her following are the variations in the ways people see information literacy:

1. Content Frame
2. Competency Frame
3. Learning to Learn Frame
4. Personal Relevance Frame
5. Social Impact Frame, and
6. Relational Frame

There are many models of information literacy. Like 'Big Six' and 'Information Search Process' models, 'Empowering 8 Model of Information Literacy' has been developed in an IFLA sponsored workshop hosted by the National Institute of Library and Information Sciences (NILIS), University of Colombo, Colombo, Sri Lanka in the year 2004. In fact, if information is fish than information literacy is the art of fishing. 'Empowering 8 Model of Information Literacy' is meant to teach the art of fishing. It is includes following eight steps:

1. Identify
2. Explore
3. Select
4. Organize
5. Create
6. Present
7. Assess, and
8. Apply

By following these eight steps, an information seeker will feel empowered by having timely access to pertinent information. There are 101 skills associated with these eight steps of the 'Empower 8 Model'. This model has been specifically developed to cater to the needs of the information seekers in the Asian region.

INFORMATION LITERACY STANDARDS

There are following five information literacy standards:

1. The information literate student determines the nature and extent of the information needed.
2. The information literate student accesses needed information effectively and efficiently.
3. The information literate student evaluates information and its sources critically and incorporates selected information into his or her knowledge base and value system.
4. The information literate student, individually or as a member of group, uses information effectively to accomplish a specific purpose.
5. The information literate student understands many of the economic, legal, and social issues surrounding the use of information and accesses and uses information ethically and legally.

Do we develop these attributes among information seekers? We must ask this question to ourselves. Perhaps we will get the answer and change our attitude. Today, the information seeker is overwhelmed by the web-based chaos and the following line by Coleridge becomes very relevant:

WATER WATER EVERYWHERE, BUT NOT A DROP TO DRINK

We must ask ourselves a question that are we competent to provide the end-user with that drop of water in the form of pertinent information. We put this question to you to find a suitable answer. LIPs must commit themselves to bridge the widening gap between the 'info-rich' and the 'info-poor' on the one hand and the growing gap between the 'tacit knowledge' and the 'explicit knowledge' on the other hand. For this, LIPs will have to develop a critical and positive outlook, as well as a learning attitude to add value to their resources and services. We had enough of talking about information literacy. Now is the time to promote the concept and practice of information literacy across frontiers.

CONCLUSION

The real power of any nation is not its money or natural resources; rather it lies with its human resources. Hence, a nation that puts premium on its human resources is bound to lead other nations. Similarly, the value of knowledge and information lies in use. Education, information literacy and lifelong learning are the three pillars for putting knowledge to work. Libraries and information networks have a pivotal role to play in human progress by preserving and serving knowledge and information across frontiers. Library and information professionals must leave no stone unturned to develop hybrid libraries that are user-centred and expert-assisted. Preservation of our documentary heritage is the hallmark of librarianship. Hence, too much bias in favour of buying access from the commercial providers as well as too much dependence on the Internet and the Google for information is not good in the end. If something goes wrong with the Internet or Google starts charging for its use, we will be in a thick use. If we are really committed to nation building then we must not promote the interests of commercial information providers at the cost of our libraries that are service agencies. There should be no compromise on quality of education and integration of information literacy to support lifelong learning and promoting the use of knowledge and information. Every effort must be made to bridge gap between the tacit knowledge and explicit knowledge. Information literacy is the best tool for as well as lifeline of lifelong learning.

REFERENCES

Andretta, Susie. *Reflecting on Six Frames of Information Literacy* www.ilit.org/ilresearch/indexilresearch.htm (Accessed on 07 January 2010)

Bruce, Christine. *Seven Faces of Information Literacy in Higher Education* sky.fit.quit.edu.au/~bruce/il/faces.jsp (Accessed on 07 January 2010)

India. National Knowledge Commission (NKC) www.**knowledgecommission**.gov.in/ *(Accessed on 26 December 2009)*

Jagtar Singh. Digital library of the future: promises, perils and models. In: *Knowledge, library and information networking (NACLIN 2009)*, edited by H.K. Kaul and V.K. Anand. New Delhi: DELNET, 2009, pp. 1-12.

Senge, Peter M. 1994. *The fifth discipline: the art and practice of the learning organization.* New York: Currency Doubledat.

UNESCO. Education for All Programme (EFAP) www.apc.org/en/.../**unescos-education-all-programme**-put-icts-practice *(Accessed on 26 December 2009)*

UNESCO. Information for All Programme (IFAP) *portal.**unesco**.org/.../ev.php-URL_ID=1627&URL_DO= DO_TOPIC&URL_SECTION=201.html (Accessed on 26 December 2009)*

UNESCO. Learning: The Treasure Within www.**unesco**.org/education/educprog/lwf/dl/**learning**2020.pdf *(Accessed on 26 December 2009)*

UN Millennium Development Goals www.un.org/**millenniumgoals**/ *(Accessed on 26 December 2009)*

2

Digital Curation and Preservation of Archival Documents and Manuscripts in India

Dr. H.S.Chopra
Librarian, Guru Nanak Dev University, Amritsar(Pb)

ABSTRACT

Millions of documents in Indian Archives and approximately 5 million manuscripts written on various forms of writing material scattered throughout India are in urgent need of digital preservation. Paper manuscripts with the passage of time are getting fragile and brittle because of various reasons. Lamination or encapsulation does not seem to be a permanent solution of preserving the cultural heritage for the posterity. Advent of information technology and telecommunication has changed the scenario of preservation as well as dissemination of information of archives and manuscripts throughout the world. OAIS Open Archival Information System is the latest system claimed to be of international standard is being advised to be adopted for archives.

India is a very rich country in ancient literature. However, this information is in various languages for which preparation of indigenous programs is essential.

Role of National Archives of India and National Mission for Manuscripts has been discussed in detail. Training courses offered by NAI need to be revised and courses like 'digital preservation', 'digital documents', 'digitization of manuscripts' 'Storage Techniques', 'On line Accessibility' etc. should be arranged at regional and university level. National Mission for Manuscripts (1994) is aiming at digitizing all the manuscripts and have a central depository. However, its terms and conditions of agreement need to be revised in order to make it successful.

Atmospheric control is one of the basic thing for digitization which we are lacking in Indian Archives and manuscript depositories. Placement of the databases in different forms at different geographical places is very essential.

There are a number of dangers to the 'digital documents', such as media, hardware, software, network failures; Obsolescence of media, software & hardware; natural disaster; external attack; economic failure and organizational decline. UNESCO is continuously emphasizing the significance of digital preservation of cultural heritage of the world in any form, for the posterity. Many of these sources having lasting value and significance should be protected as well preserved. It aims that 'information should be for all'. Climate controlled storage facility, trained staff, timely checking of different types of digital medias, change of software or hardware whenever needed, regular power supply, regular Users's orientation etc. are necessary for the proper upkeep of the 'digital documents'. Indian Universities, archives and manuscript repositories can digitize all rare documents at a nominal cost if there is encouragement from the managements and authorities as well as initiative from the staff. Thus we will not left behind in preserving the rare documents and manuscripts in digital form.

Keywords: Digital Curation, Digital Preservation; Archives; Manuscripts; Digitization; Cultural Heritage.

Albeit archives are centralised ones yet the manuscripts are scattered at various places within India as well as out side India. In India we have National Archives of India and nineteen state archives which possess millions of rare documents relating to different departments of the Centre and States. Pre-Independence documents dating back to 1748 are available in archives.[1] Archives have private papers, documents relating to different kingdoms ruled by kings during British Rule, rare books, maps, manuscripts, newspapers etc. Holdings occupy about 75,000 running feet of shelves in National Archives only.[2] National Archives has also record of 20 state agencies established by the British Government in order to have complete records of all principalities governed by Indian kings. [3]

In addition to it we have about 50 lakh(5 million) rare manuscripts.[4] All these documents need immediate digital preservation as the documents on the paper are becoming brittle and fragile day by day. So far as archives are concerned this information is available at certain places that too under Central Government or State Governments but the position of manuscripts is different as these are possessed by various types of institutions, universities, religious places and individuals.

'The greatest difficulty in digitization is its present availability, these can be in local temple or mosque, in a big library or state archive, in the private collection of a Nawab or in the small village with an individual'.

Indian civilisation is as old as the other civilisations of the Orient. [5] Various types of formats for writing were used from time to time. The manuscripts written on cloth, palm-leaves, birch bark paper etc. need immediate digital preservation so that this valueable material may become easily accessible to scholars doing research at other places through on line. Time has come to get these get protected from perishing. [6]

India has an excellent wealth of ancient literature, approximately 20% of total ancient world literature is in India.[7] Before the establishment of National Mission for Manuscripts, National Archives of India was also looking after the manuscripts. Special grants to various types of institutions were given and are still being given for conservation, preservation and restoration of manuscripts. Training courses offered by NAI need to be revised and courses like 'digital preservation', 'digital documents', 'digitization of manuscripts', 'Storage techniques', 'On line Accessibility' etc. should be arranged at regional and University level. National Mission for Manuscripts is collecting the information of all manuscripts and even of those which were publically unknown to scholars and Universities. [8] This effort is worth appreciation as a Central database of manuscripts can be prepared. Awareness among the general public about manuscripts is also being created. [9]

As most of the manuscripts are in the possession of individuals, Oriental and religious libraries, they are least interested to part away even with the digitized version of the manuscripts. Devotion, religious feelings and old attachment are other things associated with the manuscripts. Even to obtain a digital copy of manuscripts is not so easy. Catalogues prepared by universities are being ignored and new data sheets are being prepared. [10] Repetition of noting down bibliographic description can be avoided. Such money can be utilized for preservation, conservation, restoration and digitization.

Guidelines for agreement with an institution by National Mission for Manuscripts as under are not acceptable to most of the institutions for digitization :

i) The non-recurring items such as manuscripts, texts, photographs with negatives and other assets will be the property of NMM. NMM will have exclusive copyright over the materials and it will be fully entitled to use the same in any manner.

ii) The MPC Project Coordinator or the Head of the Institution shall have no claim to share any royalty and/or any other additional remuneration.

iii) NMM will have the right to short close the project at any time without assigning any reason. If, however, the project is short-closed by any Institution-MPC, Project Coordinator or the Head of the Institution for whatever reason which in the opinion of NMM is not justified, the amount of expenditure on the Project Coordinator or the Head of the Institution. The decision in this regard of the Mission Director of NMM or his/her nominee will be final and binding.

iv) All disputes, decisions and other question in any way arising out of or relating to this MOU shall be referred to the Mission Director, NMM, whose decision will be final in the matter.

v) It will be the sole prerogative of NMM to bring out publication based on the information provided by the reports submitted by any Library-MPC.

Sense of possessiveness of any rare document is a major drawback in India. Permission to have a complete digital copy may create some problems for a particular religion. Therefore, the managements and authorities become reluctant to give permission for full version, digitization or Xeroxing or Microfilming.

In India the manuscript repositories may have to face displeasures in some cases because of comments regarding other faiths. When 'Faith' is shaken the problem starts. Availability of full text of manuscripts freely accessible may produce counter results in some cases. [11]

These digital repositories will require the basic infrastructure like computers, scanners, digital camera etc. Indian Institutions possessing such material can afford to have the basic infrastructure for digitization. There is no lack of computer professionals. [12] This material is not to be used by the architects or managers of these digital repositories but by teachers, researchers and scholars.

DIGITAL CURATION

It is a fact that digital information after some years degrades, computing platforms, programming languages, formats, applications will change sufficiently overtime. Some institutions may start digitization of rare documents but after completing the project, if left unattended it may cause a big loss on finding the CDs/DVDs are corrupted ones.

Curation is the activity of maintaining a body of information so that it remains usable overtime. Curation covers the entire life cycle of the information from curation to use and from archival to use.

The following steps are taken in digital curation :-

i) Selection

ii) Appraisal

iii) Capture of metadata

iv) Conversion of documents to archival format

v) Documents dealing with different disciplines to be converted to archival format

vi) authenticity

vii) Annotation and linkage

IMPORTANCE OF DATA

Scientists and researchers produce large amounts of digital data which needs to be digitized for use or sale in future. This trend indicates that such scientific records and documents are at risk from technology obsolescence and from the fragility of digital media. Digital curation is a new phrase that includes data archiving and digital preservation but also goes beyond that to include the active management and appraisal of data over the life-cycle of scholarly and scientific interest.

Migration : The migration of digital information refers to the periodic transfer of digital materials from one hardware and software configuration to another, or from one generation of computer technology to a subsequent generation. The motive of migration is to preserve the integrity of digital objects and to retain the ability of users to retrieve, display, and use them in the face of continuously changing computer technology.

The Open Archiving Information System(OAIS) model developed by the Consultative Committee for Space Data Systems(CCSDS), breaks migration into four categories: refreshment, replication, repackaging, and transformation. Refreshment ensures that a reliable copy of the bit stream of a digital object is maintained while replication and repackaging ensure that a manageable package of the object is available. On the other hand, transformation actually modifies the bit stream of a digital object and this is what is considered in the process of migration.

Rather than focus on the technology, information migration tends to focus on the intellectual content and on ensuring its accessibility using current technology. This strategy could be facilitated through copying the digital information to an analog medium or through application programs that are backward compatible. It could also be facilitated through the conversion to digital resources into a small number of standard formats that are hardware and software independent.

The second solution, software that is backward compatible, will simplify migration. The latest versions of most popular word processing packages, for example, will be able to decode files created on earlier version of the same package. Another approach entails initially migrating digital information from the great multiplicity of formats to a smaller more manageable number of standard formats.

There are a variety of migration strategies: Minimum migration, preservation migration, recreation human conversion migration, and automatic conversion migration. Recently, the concept of migration on request has been conceived by the consortium of University Research Libraries Exemplars for Digital Archives(CEDARS) project, in which original objects are maintained and preserved in addition to a migration tool that runs on a current computing platform and can be employed by users as necessary. Key to successful migration is the knowledge of the original data format and a close match in functionality between the original and replacement format.

In case information belongs to different types, digital curation requirements also change. After sometime many textual and multimedia documents may only need to be migrated to new formats as older formats fall out of favour.

Emulation

Given the problems just outlined, the dominant approach to digital preservation has been that of migration. Migration is the process of transferring data from a platform that is in danger of becoming obsolete to a current platform. This process has both dangers and costs. The notable danger is that of data loss, or in some cases the loss of original functionality or the 'look and feel' of the original platform. For these reasons some have seen emulation as an alternative and superior strategy. The essential idea behind emulation is to be able to access or run original data/ software on a new/current platform by running software on the new/current platform that emulates the original platform.

Technical approaches

If emulation is to be adopted, the firm question is what is to be emulated? Three options are:

- Emulate applications
- Emulate operating systems
- Emulate hardware platforms

Content : It is here that emulation has its strongest attraction. One of the issues for digital preservation is what needs to be preserved in addition to the pure intelectual content of a digital object. In some cases the 'look and feel' of a digital object may be important, as may its interactivity. The fear is that migration to new platforms may lose these aspects, and that emulation may be the only strategy for preserving them. This problem is exacerbated, of course, by the increasing use of more complex digital objects (multimedia and hypermedia). Intellectual Property Rights(IPR) issues may well be involved in emulating either operating systems or applications. It seems almost certain that the cost of emulation will mean that emulation will not(if unsupported) be an option for every user. This will be one part of a case for wanting trusted organisations that can undertake the work and make this available for other to use.

RELIANCE ON COMPUTER MUSEUMS

The idea that computer museums be established, where old machines would run original software to access to obsolete documents(Swade 1998) is highly problematic for several reasons.

Old digital documents and the original software needed to access them will rarely survive on their original digital media. The obsolete document would therefore have to be read by an obsolete machine from a new medium for which that machine has no physical drive, no interface, and no device software. The museum approach would therefore require building unique new device interfaces between every new medium and every obsolete computer in the museum as new storage media evolve, as well as coding driver software for these devices, which would demand maintaining programming skills for each obsolete machine.

In his report at least, Rothenberg is extremely scathing about migration. He provides a whole list of reasons why he believes migration to be inadequate as a preservation strategy. Rothenberg states that migration is:

- Labour intensive
- Time-consuming
- Expensive
- Error-prone
- Risky (causing lost or corrupted information)
- Non-scalable
- and that migration can require new solutions for each new format.

HOW SHOULD EMULATION BE ACHIEVED?

1. Developing generalizable techniques for specifying emulator that will run on unknown future computers and that capture all of those attributes required to recreate the behavior of current and future digital documents;
2. Developing techniques for saving — in human-readable

form—the metadata needed to find, access, and recreate digital documents so that emulation techniques can be used for preservation; and

3. Developing techniques for encapsulating documents, their attendant metadata, software, and emulator specifications in ways that ensure their cohesion and prevent their corruption.

INTERNATIONAL SCENE

Latest Software for Archives

OAIS : It is an Open Archival Information System developed by the consultative committee for Space Data Systems and adopted as ISO 14721 : 2003. OAIS is meant for an archive, consisting of an organization of people and systems, that has accepted the responsibility to preserve information and make it available for a designated community.

This reference model addresses a full range of archival information preservation including ingest, archival storage, data management, access, and dissemination. It also addresses the migration of digital information to new media and forms, the data models used to represent the information, the role of software in information preservation, and the exchange of digital information among archives. It identifies both internal and external interfaces to the archive functions, and it identifies a number of high-level services at these interfaces. It provides various illustrative examples and some "best practice" recommendations. It defines a minimal set of responsibilities for and archive to be called an OAIS, and it also defines a maximal archive to provide a broad set of useful terms and concepts.

The OAIS model described in ISO 14721:2003 may be

applicable to any archive. It is specifically applicable to organization with responsibility of making information available for the long term. This includes organizations with other responsibilities, such as processing and distribution in response to programmatic needs.[13]

India is a multilingual country. Therefore, archives as well as manuscripts are in different languages which may not be able to properly use OAIS, and indigenous softwares will be required.

The archival records are used for various purposes and also as a resource material for a number of subjects and particularly for the study of history and historical trends in a particular period. Among all records being created in our public, semi-public and private organizations, paper-records still form the most common medium. Archival records are being laminated for preservation. [14] How far these will survive? Similarly our digitization program will need our continuous attention for making the infrastructure updated. We have seen longevity of paper but of electronic media it is yet to be seen.

Functional Model for an Archive

Ingest (Accession)

Archival Storage

Data Management : Meta data

Administration

Preservation Planning

Access

User's Satisfaction

Threats

The following dangers can be anticipated to the digital Archives and Manuscript depositories.

(I) **Media Failure:** There can be change in storage media, every media is changing very fast thus during upgradation there can be irrecoverable bit-errors, disk crash and loss of off-line media.

(II) Hardware Failure

(III) Software Failure

(IV) Communication Errors

(V) Failure of Network Services

(VI) Media and Hardware Obsolescence

(VII) Software Obsolescence

(VIII) Operator Error

(IX) Nature Disaster

(X) External (Virus) Attack

(XI) Economic Draught

(XII) Organisational Decline

Diversity is very essential to preserve the digital documents. Some documents are born-digital whereas others are digitized. Most systems use off-line media to provide diversity in media for storing replicas, and to isolate some replicas as far as possible from network-borne-threats. We can have these at various Geographical places in order to avoid any catastrophe. Diversity of softwares will also be in the interest of any institution. [15]

Any information dealing with particular time, place or person should be digitized in such a way that the user can access it and it should be authentic, authoritative, reliable and purposeful.

So far as cost-effectiveness is concerned we have already basic infrastructure in universities and archives. The only thing is the initiative from staff and management of libraries and Archives. The major libraries which are possessing a large number of manuscripts should start digitization as the manuscripts on paper are slowly and slowly getting deteriorated because of various factors such as environmental, micro biological agents, acidity, humidity, radiant energy, accidental agents etc. Now instead of lamination, encapsulation is being preferred.

DIGITAL CURATION OF INDIAN CULTURAL HERITAGE

Digital information and services have changed almost the complete academic scenario. ICT and change have become synonymous words. Mode of availability of all resources in academic field have undergone a major change. The scholars all the world over now expect to save the contents of documentary heritage in digital form.

India is one of the oldest civilizations of the world. The manuscripts are on various forms of writing. According to an estimate twenty percent of the total manuscripts of the world are in India. Since 1994 National Mission for Manuscripts is working in this respect. Manuscripts which are on various forms of writing are nearing extinction. Earlier lamination, with the help of cellulose acetate foil and tissue paper, was considered as safe. Technology to preserve the manuscripts. Now, The latest research has proved that it will damage the manuscript after few years. In the age of ICT digitization is being considered as the best solution to preserve the brittle, fragile and decaying manuscripts. Images of some of the writing materials like leaves, bark of the plants, cloth, wood etc. need immediate preservation in digital form. These manuscripts cannot last even two or three centuries.

With the passage of time all the documents, objects, buildings will face an extinction for ever. Traditional approach to save all the objects, documents are for a temporary phase and not for posterity.

In the present age of ICT digitization is one of the best solution to preserve the images of manuscripts, rare books, maps, paintings etc. Such full text digitization can be put on Net as well as saved in DVD's for future generations.

National Archives of India and many State Archives are still following the traditional measures to preserve, conserve and restore the manuscripts and other brittle documents written on various forms of writing. Birch bark and palm leaf were two very important forms of writing in ancient and medieval India, Scholars during ancient times used to preserve their manuscripts by using Ghora bach, neem leaves, leaves of Margosa tree, pandri grass. Our ancestors saved their writings for hundred of years for future generations.

So far as digitization is concerned it has almost swept away all the educational institutions in India. Most of the universities have started digitizing their manuscripts and rare documents. However, the basic thing is Digital Curation i.e. how to preserve the digital material.

INFLIBNET

Recently U.G.C.(India) has made compulsory for all the universities to submit one soft copy of every M.Phil. dissertation and Ph.D. thesis to Inflibnet centre located at Ahmedabad(Gujrat). Inflibnet will upload full texts of all dissertations and theses on Net so that researchers, teachers throughout the world may be able to access it. It is an important step as full text is being made available free of cost. It is presumed that it will stop plagarism in research. In order to check plagarism all the universities are supposed to co-operate this project. Inflibnet centre will have to be very careful about the safety, security, accessibility of the contents. It would have been better if in the initial stage an abstract, contents and introduction would have been made freely accessible. UMI and other institutions in developed countries are not offering the Ph.D. theses or dissertations free of cost. ProQuest while giving access to database of theses charges a significant amount. Inflibnet centre will have to take responsibility to save the data as well as adopt long term plans to change the format of media.

Indra Gandhi National Centre for the Arts is moving with the times. It has strived very heard to save the documentary as well as cultural heritage of India. IGNCA values both folk, classic, oral, written or oral, ancient or modern document or object of cultural heritage. IGNCA is the nodal agency for creation of a data bank on cultural heritage in any form, National Mission for Manuscripts and National Mission of Intangible cultural Heritage. IGNCA has also got recognition from UNESCO as a nodal agency for the development of regional database for South and South East Asian Countries on art, cultural heritage and life-styles through the application of state of the art technologies for standardization, exchange and dissemination of data.

KALASAMPDA DIGITAL LIBRARY : RESOURCES OF INDIAN CULTURAL HERITAGE

Kalasampda facilitates the scholars to access and view the materials including over couple of lakhs of manuscripts, slides, rare books, photographs, audio and video along with highly researched publications, from a single window. Multimedia computer technology has been used to integrate variety of cultural information accessible at one place. The system aims at being a digital repository of content and information with a user- friendly interface. The knowledge base such created may help the scholars to explore and visualize the information stored in multiple layers. The facility is currently available only on Internet. Although, the partial information can be accessed from the IGNCA's official website. www.ignca.gov.in, uploaded with necessary approvals.

Today, the services are totally dependent on the digital contents and long term preservation of the data becomes crucial for the institutions. Periodic migration of the data, keeping multiple copies of the same contents etc. should be considered for the uninterrupted services to the scholars and artists.

IGNCA in the initial could not save the data as proper attention was not given to have backup of data. Moreover, data was not properly migrated on the new platform. In order to save the data, and to check the wastage of human labour and money long term plans are essential. IGNCA should consult the Digital curation centres in the other countries. Centre should have policy for data migration.

Suggestion : All the institutions should generate the information in digital form, moreover, it should be as per the archival standards or formats. Institution managers must understand that dissemination should be in digital form. Digital data must have multiple copies with a copy in National Digital Archives for Security.

For the long term preservation of digital data there should be National Digital Archives as well as State Archives. These archives should undertake the responsibility of preservation of data. It should be capable to migrate data from one media to another media and also from one format to another format. There should be a national digital policy so that the digital data generated or going to be generated by all the archives, institutions, educational institutions manuscript depositories etc. should be kept safely.

ROLE OF UNESCO

The digital heritage consists of unique resources of human knowledge and expression. It embraces cultural, educational, scientific and administrative resources, as well as technical, legal, medical and other kinds of information created digitally, or converted into digital form from existing analogue resources. Where resources are "born digital", there is no other format but the digital object.

Digital materials include texts, databases, still and moving images, audio, graphics, software and web pages, among a wide and growing range of formats. They are frequently ephemeral, and require purposeful production, maintenance and management to be retained.

Many of these resources have lasting value and significance, and therefore constitute a heritage that should be protected and preserved for current and future generations. This ever-growing heritage may exist in any language, in any part of the world, and in any area of human knowledge or expression.

The purpose of preserving the digital heritage is to ensure that it remains accessible to the public. Accordingly, access to digital heritage materials, especially those in the public domain, should be free from unreasonable restrictions. At the same time, sensitive and personal information should be protected from any form of intrusion.

The world's digital heritage is at risk of being lost to posterity. Contributing factors include the rapid obsolescene of the hardware and software which brings it to life, uncertainties about resources, responsibility and methods for maintenance and preservation, and the lack of supportive legislation.

Attitudinal change has fallen behind technological change. Digital evolution has been too rapid and costly for governments and institutions to develop timely and informed preservation strategies. The threat to the economic, social, intellectual and cultural potential of the heritage- the building blocks of the future- has not been fully grasped. [16]

a) urge hardware and software developers, creators, publishers and distributors of digital materials as well as other private sector partners to cooperate with national libraries, archives, museums and other public heritage organizations in preserving the digital heritage;

b) develop training and research, and share experience and knowledge among the institutions and professional associations concerned;

c) encourage universities and other research organizations, both public and private, to ensure preservation of research data.

Preservation of the digital heritage requires sustained efforts on the part of governments, creators, publishers, relevant industries and heritage institutions. In the face of the current digital divide, it is necessary to reinforce international cooperation and solidarity to enable all countries to ensure creation, dissemination, preservation and continued accessibility of their digital heritage. Industries, publishers and mass communication media are urged to promote and share knowledge and technical expertise. [17]

CLIMATE CONTROLLED STORAGE FACILITY

Digital Preservation requires climate controlled media storage facility. In India we face severe heat, dampness, cold atmosphere in North, humidity and stormy winds which are harmful to digital data, manuscripts and archives. Digital Section or Digital Library of archives and manuscripts should be fully air-conditioned. Provision for uninterrupted power supply is very essential. Any wrong attempt to preserve these digitized documents may jeopardise the whole exercise in vain. Controlled atmosphere is no problem in Indian Universities. State Archives can also afford this facility. Every digital library should follow one standard. National Mission for Manuscripts has prepared a standard Manus Sheet for the preparation of bibliographic discription of manuscript. However, there should be full proof security for the protection of digitized material. The institutions should be capable enough to adopt the new techniques and software.

Environment control should be regularly checked. Staff should periodically inspect and see that higher risk items have not yet reached advanced stages of decay. Software upgrades and hardware replacements are scheduled at longer intervals. Digitization has become essential for Indian manuscripts and archival records.

Now the problem is to be solved by computer scientists that digitized material should be safe for posterity.

REFERENCES

1. Low, D.A. , 1969. ***Government Archives in South Asia***, Cambridge, Cambridge University Press, p.32.
2. Loc.cit.
3. Ibid., pp.196-225.
4. **National Mission for Manuscripts**,. Report of the Second year 2004-2005. p.7.
5. Durant, W., 1954. ***The Story of civilization; part I : Our Oriental Heritage***, Newyork, Simon and Schuster, p.394.
6. Chakraborti, M.L., 1975. ***Bibliography in theory and practice***, Calcutta(Kolkatta), The World Press, pp.28-39.
7. Durant, W., 1954. ***The Story of Civilization; part I: Our Oriental Heritage***, New York, Simon and Schuster, p.555.

8. **National Mission for Manuscripts,** Report of the Second year 2004-2005. pp.6,12.

9. Op.cit., p.12.

10. Op.cit., p.10.

11. Some manuscripts relate to dissent groups of major faiths which sometimes show disrespect to the 'Primary Faith' Punjabi manuscripts relating to Sikh religion face this problem.

12. **Every year India is producing 3.50 lakh computer professionals in India,** The Hindustan Times, March 5, 2006.

13. Michael Day, ***'The OAIS Reference Model'; current implementations'*** http://www-ukoln-ac.uk/ Accessed on 20/04/2006.

14. Now Encapsulation is being favoured for preserving manuscripts instead of lamination.

15. David, S.H. Rosenthal and others, **Requirements for Digital Preservation Systems,** http://www.dlib.or/dlib/november 05/ rosenthal/11 rosenthal.html. Accessed on 25/04/2006

16. **Unesco documents and Publications** http://unesdoc.unesco.or/ulis/faq/html Accessed on 25/04/2006

17. Loc cit.

3

Library Automation

Dr. D.K. Kaushik

Principal, Manohar Memorial College, Fatehabad

Haryana - 125050

ABSTRACT

Now-a-days Information and Communication Technologies (ICT) has also made a deep impact on the functioning and management of libraries in Institutions. The author in the present article has made an attempt to discuss the overall view of the library automation. Originality is not claimed here as it is just a review article, which will help the librarians to go for the library automation work in their libraries where libraries are not computerised. The fear that the library staff has to undergo extensive training is ruled out as a little computer knowledge will solve the purpose. Further it is not very expensive and a very small one time investment for the purchase of computers, software and other interfacing device will be enough for the automation work. It will also save time for the circulation of the documents and for preparation of inventory report.

INTRODUCTION

Library in fact is the collection of books/materials used for common person, which is housed in the room or building. The library can be maintained or organised by a public body, an institution or a private person. Libraries also provide a place for studying in a very congenial and peaceful environment. The variety of books and materials including rare collection of books are generally available in the library intended for use by people who choose not to /or cannot afford to procure extensive collection of books. The traditional libraries have been focussing for long on the preservation and management of content in physical form. Further the traditional libraries are limited by cost and storage space.

In this modern world, computers are very essential and necessary to work any type of job. It is being the most wonderful tool ever invented enables us to express our creativity. Computer's hardware and software work together to help in meeting one's computing needs, whether it is used of a word processor to write a letter or a spreadsheet to analyse the data or monitoring, planning, evaluation and management of office work.

Invention of this tool has been made possible mainly due to rapid pace of technology of the recent times. As compared to technological advancement of the developed countries through computers is no more considered as an ultra-modern technology, yet, to a common man it sounds too fascinating and something that can solve all the present problems.

This is human nature to criticise and have negative apprehensions whenever a new innovation comes into being. New things - a technology or an idea - are not easily and readily acceptable to the society, as masses are ignorant of the utility or importance of the same. However, history has shown it time and again, that, after some initial hick-ups, changes, if forceful and constant in nature are accepted and later become an essential part of life. The computers are no exception to it. Following myths existed about computers. Some of them have vanished with passage of time but some still remain in the minds of new learners.

People's apprehension that computers being very fast, quick and efficient in disposal of work, will make already employed manpower redundant is wrong. Labour hours saved by computers can be put to more productive use and further sphere of the work can also be expanded. That mass scale use of computers increases efficiency and also do not make redundant the already employed manpower, which has been proved beyond doubts by computerisation of any type of work in office/ industries.

LIBRARY AUTOMATION

So in the era of computers Library Automation help to improve the present management system of the library to pace the latest requirements of the users. We live in an information age, and libraries are expected to use Information and Communication Technologies (ICT) to provide information more expeditiously and exhaustively than before. Computerization of library "housekeeping" operations is an important activity in this context. "Automation," when used in a library or similar environment, refers to the computerization or mechanization of activities. For library Automation, following major levels of library management system are to be taken care of:

- Library Management
- House keeping operations
- Library Networking
- Development of CD-ROM library / products

- Internet facility

The library catalogue or index to the collection of books in the library forms the base for most of the library activities such as acquisition, reference, bibliographic service, inter-library loan, CAS/SDI, Documentation service etc. For the library automation the database for the collection of books in the library is made available in the network environment through computers, so that the library users can have the simultaneous access to the database. Once a database with all the details is developed, the same data can be used for circulation activities. This will eliminate the cumbersome job of printing or writing the cards and their filing at proper place in the catalogue boxes. This conserves space and saves stationary and time.

The second thing to be taken care for the library automation is use of software which can handle all the housekeeping operations of the library such as acquisition, circulation and serial control. The database of the library book or other materials should be in such a format that can be handled properly by the software used for the purpose of housekeeping operations of the library. For this, proper networking of the computers within the library should be done. The networking can also be extended to the existing network of the institution. Networking of computers within a library or organization helps the users to browse the cataloguing system from any of the workstation/ terminal. User-friendly range of software products which can streamline the library management for automation are available in the market at the nominal rates with different facilities. The software can also be got developed as per the requirement of the library from some software company. The software so developed should be in ISO 2709 format so that if at later stage one decides to go in for other software, data transfer can easily be done.

For the selection of right software for housekeeping operation librarian should keep in mind the following points:

1. The software developed by an individual or by some reputed company should have the facility to import bibliographic data available, in ISO 2709 format so that the data can be transferred to other software if need arises. Such data may, therefore, be interfaced with the website.

2. The software should be compatible with major operating systems such as WINDOWS, LINUX etc.

3. The software should be user-friendly so that minimum training and guidance is needed after installation.

4. The software should cover all the parameters required for the library and should have the multiuser facility.

The other technology which libraries can make use is the Development of CD-ROMs library products. There are many CD-ROMs available with multimedia effects on different subjects/topics. The collection of such CDs not only conserves space but also provides readymade data/ information in most practical and presentable form for the users. It can be accessed by multi-users with the help of the networking available in the library.

The next most important aspect of automation of libraries is the internet facilities. The broad band internet connection should also be made available in the library so as the user may go through e-journals and e-books on different websites. If the library subscribes these journals/books in the library which are available either free of cost or for a nominal annual fee. In addition, many academic and research institutes have also provided free access to their research papers. More use of books/Journals and other information in the digital format will lead to the digital library.

For fully automation of the library, circulation activities are also to be considered. It comprises of the following things:

- Issue, Return and the Renewal of Documents
- Report Generation
- Reminders

Once the data base for the software of library automation is prepared and installed on the computers of the library, one can use the issue, return and renewal of the books and other documents for the library in a very systematic manner. For this purpose Bar Code system is used. A Bar Code is an optical machine readable representation of data, which shows the data about the books or journals to which the bar codes are attached. Bar codes generally represent the data by varying the width and spacing of parallel lines. Bar Code generator is used to generate the bar code data for each book and journals to be attached with the documents. The Bar Codes are also generated for the membership/smart cards. Cataloguing of the books is done with the help of the library software. This is known as Online Public Access Cataloguing (OPAC). It makes the availability of books very easy and time saving.

For the transaction of the documents a Bar Code reader is interfaced to the computer at the issue counter of the library. Bar Code reader extracts information optically from the Bar Codes. The bar code when illuminated reflected light is detected by electro optical sensor attached with the Bar Code reader. The intensity of reflected light from the dark bars is less than that of the spaces. Reflected light is converted into electrical voltage signal for each bar code. The analog voltages are then converted to digital data. The software from the database gives the character data (Bibliographic details of the document) corresponding to this digital data. With the help of membership/smart card, the transaction of the documents and theft detection is possible at the counter without any error. This process is basically a direct communication between the computers of the library, library's staff and the users. It reduces cost and saves time for issue and return of the documents in the library.

In addition of circulation activities, the software may also generate daily report of the documents issued and returned. Provision may also be made for the generation of fine receipt as well the report of the fine collected day wise or month wise.

Reminders to delinquent borrowers of the documents may also be generated with the help of the library software so that the reminders may be sent to the borrowers either manually or through the email.

The new advancement in the field is the use of RFID (Radio Frequency Identification) in place of Bar Code system. RFID system is more efficient and prompt and has more flexibility, but it is more costly. The big university libraries have adopted this system.

CONCLUSION

This article gives some idea for beginners for library automation. The librarians have to pace with the latest technologies and other interfacing products available in the market for use in the automation work. It is necessary for librarians to keep a watch on the recent developments and efforts be made to provide the proper and up-to-date documents to the users. For this librarians should have the basic knowledge of the computers in addition they should interact with the computer professionals.

4

Broadcasting Medias for Digital Contents on Web

Dr. Dinesh K. Gupta
Chairman & Associate Professor,
Dept. of Lib. & Inf. Sc.,
Kurukshetra University, Kurukshetra

Ms. Veerbala
Research Scholar, Dept. of Lib. & Inf. Sc.,
Kurukshetra University, Kurukshetra

ABSTRACT

Internet has changed the communication and broadcasting trends considerably during last a couple of years. Global communication is possible in various forms and has become much faster and easier also. There are different ways of broadcasting textual, audio and video contents (digital contents) over Internet. Consequently, this technology has enabled everyone on the net apart from a mere consumer of information, to play the role of a creator, producer and disseminator of information himself without anybody else's interference; however, most of the Internet users are unaware of such facilities. Thus this article explores and highlights various broadcasting medias available over the Internet, e.g. Podcasting, Autocasting, Blogcasting,

Voicecasting and Mobliecasting etc. In the present scenario of shrinking users from the libraries, libraries can reach to the users by introduce new services and enriching existing services with the help of these communication medias.

INTRODUCTION

Communication is the process of imparting/ interchanging of thoughts and opinions through various medias e.g. textual, audio, video, images etc. Communication is a constant process throughout our lives both professionally and personally. Today, everyone enjoys the convenience of technological devices such as cell phones, computers, i-pads, i-pods, notebooks, faxes etc. which allow us to communicate globally within seconds. However, Internet is the most popular form of communication at present in society due to its ability to interact globally from any location. The Internet has changed broadcast media in a most intriguing way.

It has enabled everyone to create, produce and share one's opinions, music, videos, thoughts etc. The most interesting part of the Internet is that it has made all these mediums readily available 24x7 as long as one has Internet connection. It seems to be taking over broadcast media in terms of popularity and effective communication.

Broadcast media used to mean "sowing of seeds" over a wide field. Broadcasting is considered as a form of media that aims to reach a large audience. The social impact of broadcasting has been huge. It has had a great affect on communication and dissemination of information. The trends of broadcasting are changing very fast due to the development and convergence of digital technology.

There are several different ways of broadcasting audio and video contents (digital contents) over the Internet e.g. Podcasting, Autocasting, Blogcasting, Voicecasting and

Mobliecasting etc. Anyone create contents on his/her computer and can broadcast it using RSS to over the Internet. So, millions of people can use that contents. In this way, everyone can play the role of a creator, producer and disseminator of information himself/herself.

BROADCASTING MEDIAS OVER WEB

1. Podcasting : A podcast is a series of digital media files (either audio or video) that broadcast over the web and broken up into parts or episode. Most podcasts are similar to news radio programs and deliver information on a regular basis. Podcasts are most popular on Apple's iPod and iPhone devices, hence the name podcast, but a podcast can be enjoyed from a number of different sources and can even be listened to directly on a computer. According to Wikipedia- Podcasting is a portmanteau of the words "Pod" an acronym for "Playable On Demand" and "Broadcasting". Podcasting refers to the entire process of creating the podcast [audio], editing and publishing to the web via RSS. Podcasts are digital media files (most often audio, but they can be video as well), which are produced in a series. You can subscribe to a series of files or podcast, by using a piece of software called a ***Podcatcher*** (is an application you can use to subscribe to podcasts). Once you subscribe, your ***Podcatcher*** periodically checks to see if any new files have been published and if so, automatically downloads them onto your computer or portable music player for you to listen to or watch, whenever you wish. Podcasting is the base of the different broadcasting medias.

2. Blogcasting: A blogcast or popularly called blog is the combination of a blog post and an audio broadcast (commonly known as Podcast). According to Deletionpedia "A blogcast is an individual blog post or article with an attached audio and/or video file associated with it immediately available for downloading to any mp3 player, Web browser, or RSS reader". Excluding a few search engines like ***Blinkx***, most cannot index audio content. Therefore, some podcasters attach a transcript of the podcast to their blog so that both human beings and search engines read [and index] what is there inside the podcast show.

Libraries are using Blogs as a way to share information, to encourage feedback from their patrons, to highlight services, news, post students/faculty book reviews, issue reminders, book reservation reminders and invite comments, announce events, list new acquisitions, etc. Blog can be a wonderful marketing tool and a fantastic way to become more approachable to library users. It is all about inviting opinions and getting input from library users to collaborate on making library the best that it can be. Blogs are a simple and efficient way for librarians to stay informed and for libraries to disseminate information in a timely manner.

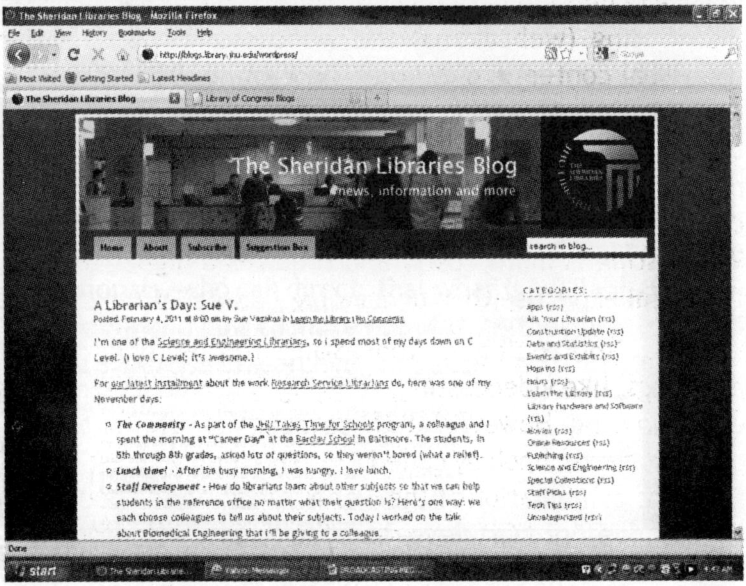

Fig. 1. Screen Shot of Sheridan Libraries' Blog

3. Autocasting : Autocast an automated form of podcast that automatically converts the text on a blog into speech so that it can be downloaded as a podcast and it can be synchronized into a portable audio device, or played on a desktop computer. The only difference being that the audio is not narrated by a human being but it has been generated automatically from the blog feed using a text to speech conversion engine. ***Talkr*** is one such autocast service that converts the text inside RSS feeds to podcasts.

4. Webcasting : Webcasting is the method of broadcasting live audio and video in real-time, to audiences all over the world via the Internet. Sometimes it is also called Streaming. It is a way to distribute a recording of a class or event over the Internet. This is video and/or audio of a class or event that user can view live on his/her desktop or laptop computer using a Flash media player. All live classes or events can be archived for viewing on-demand anywhere, anytime. Webcast clients allow a user to connect to a server, which is distributing (webcasting) the webcast and displays the televisual contents to the user. Podcasting and webcasting are both ways of putting audio contents on the Internet, but the delivery methods of the audio are different. With podcasting a listener downloads the audio on to his or her computer, but with webcasting audio is streaming. Webcasting is more costly and requires a higher level of technical expertise than podcasting.

5. Vodcasting : Vodcasting has actually other meanings, like videocasting, vlogging, video podcasting and videoblogging. However, all these meanings refer to the use of the same technology called RSS. The term vodcast comes from the combination of the words "video" and "podcast". *Vodcast* is a used for delivering "Video On Demand" (VOD) files online via RSS feeds. A step beyond podcasting, vodcasting adds video to the downloadable sound files for users. Users can download the video files after subscribing a vodcast in one of the many freely available directory programs. After downloading and saving them to a portable video player, users can choose when and where they want to watch the video. Vodcasting means creating and distributing video podcasts. Unlike Podcasting where user only requires a microphone, for creating Vodcasts user needs a video camera and video editing software like ***Sony Vegas, Adobe Premiere*** or ***Apple Final Cutpro***.

6. CourseCasting : CourseCasting helps the students to take the lecture with them wherever they go. Based on Podcasting technology, CourseCasting give students the ability to listen lectures or supplemental material from participating courses. CourseCasting allows teachers to record their lectures either on their computer or on an MP3 player, upload the audio files (and possibly slides, pictures, or even videos) to a site where students can download the lecture to their own MP3 players. (Most frequently used Apple's iPod.) The methods of distribution vary, but generally

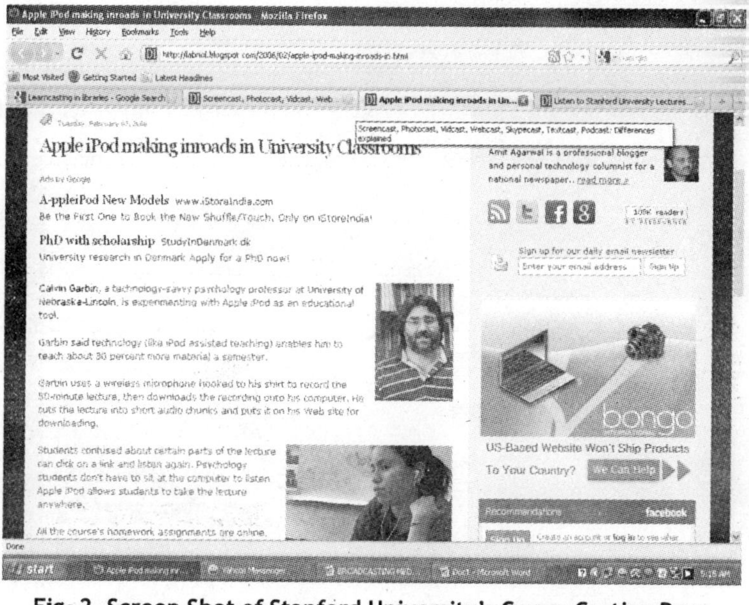

Fig. 2. Screen Shot of Stanford University's CourseCasting Page

universities are setting up their own secure sites where students must log in to download lectures specific to their schedule (i.e., it is usually not possible to get free lectures from a course you haven't paid for.) CourseCasting also features recordings of campus activities such as poetry readings, lecture series, special topics etc.

7. LearnCasting : LearnCasting is a category of podcasting or even vodcasting that aims deliver educational contents. Learncast is online educational or instructional contents, which may be delivered via a podcast or a syndication feed such as RSS. Learncast offers an expanding range of high-quality educational videos and associated interactive contents. It provides live streaming events with interactive components, pre-recorded and programmed events and access to video on demand. Stanford University professors are already putting their lectures on iTunes. It is also known as podagogy (*Podagogy* is the art or science of using Podcasts for educational purposes).

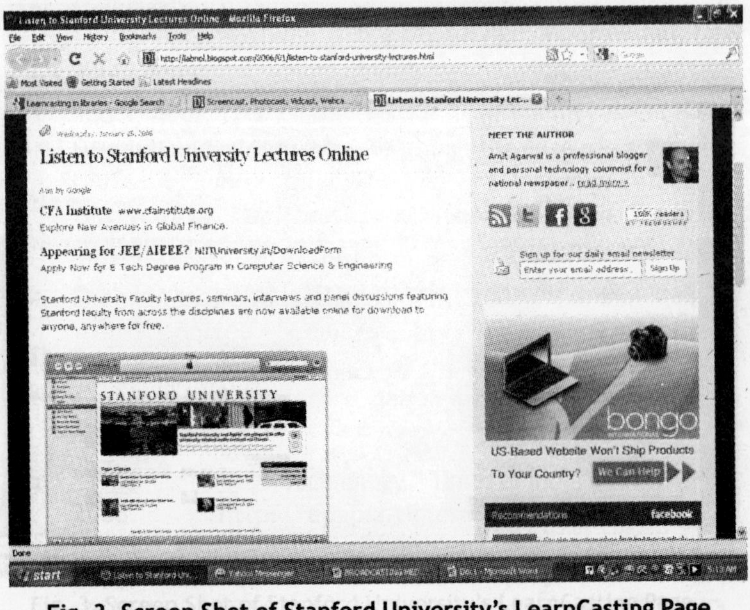

Fig. 3. Screen Shot of Stanford University's LearnCasting Page

8. Photocasting : Photocasting is very similar to the much hyped podcasting except that the contents being syndicated are specifically photos. Photocasting is a new way of sharing photos accompanied by music or narrations. It is like sending a photo album to friends and family, and getting them changed automatically on their computers when creator updates them. When someone subscribes to your photos [photocasts], he will see them in their iPhoto library just as you see them in yours. ***Flickr*** is one example of Photocast. This can be used in libraries for virtual tours, promote the events and books, share the events and historical images of library etc.

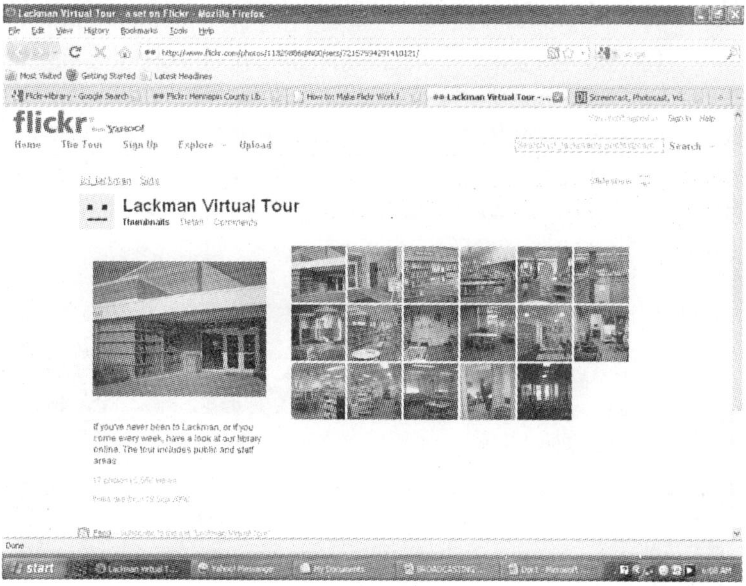

Fig. 4. Screen Shot of PhotoCasting Page

9. Slidecasting: A slidecast is a term that is used to describe an audio podcast that is combined with a slideshow presentation. It is similar to a video podcast in that it combines dynamically generated image with audio synchronization, but it is different in that it uses presentation software, such as PowerPoint, to create the image and the sequence of display separately from the time of the audio podcast's original recording. Slidecasting may be useful for the display of relevant photographs or text and are an alternative to camera video recordings. It is the online distribution and syndication of video recordings of live slideshow presentations and accompanying narrations. Everyone can use ***SildeShare*** for creating all sorts of slideshows and audio files can also be add with them about anything like- songs, musicals, recorded talks, voice narrations, instrumental music, talk shows, podcast interviews, news bulletins, speeches, advertising jingles et al.

10. Sceencasting: A screencast is nothing but a screen recording accompanied by an audio commentary done by the screencaster explaining what is happening on the screen as it happens and distributed through RSS. A screencast is like

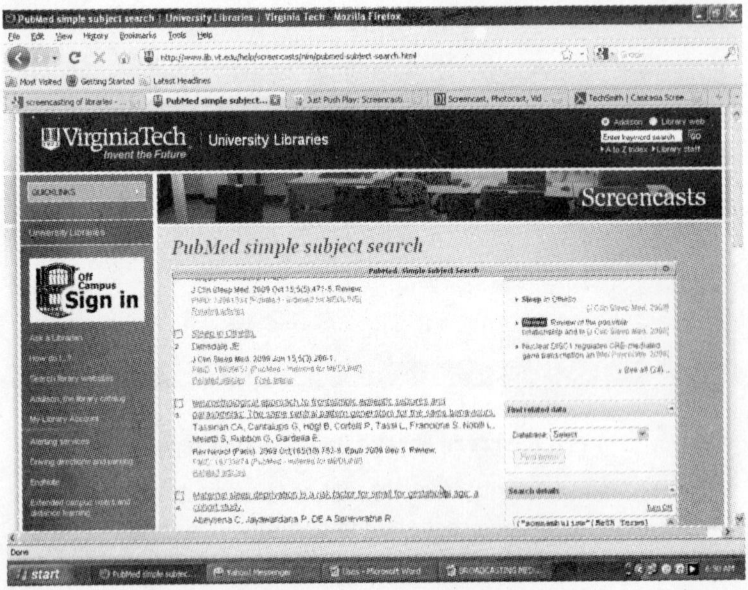

Fig. 5. Screen Shot of a ScreenCasting Page

a movie that captures the display from a computer screen along with someone talking about, what is being shown. This might take the form of a formal narrated Powerpoint presentation, a software demo, or an informal walk-through of a particular concept. Software like ***Techsmith-Camtasia Studio*** is used for creating screencasts. It can be used in libraries for user orientations regarding how to use the library resources effectively and efficiently. It also reduces the workload of the staff for repeated users' queries for searching the resources of library.

11. Textcasting : Textcasting is a term coined by American online Magazine ***Slate***. Just like Blogcasting. It is like a podcast which user can download to either i-tunes or i-pod, but rather than listening to it, user can read it. User can download a lengthy mp3 file as per a normal podcast. The difference is that the podcast mp3 is silent in textcasting means it delivered text to your iPod rather than audio. The textcast itself comes in the accompanying description, held in the podcast xml RSS feed. The text of the download textcast is readable as long as user's silent mp3 is playing. User can subscribe textcast feed like other podcasts. e.g ***Slate*** magazine can deliver textcast to your iPod in a small file containing the full text of that day's summary of the top stories from the US best newspapers.

12. Mobilecasting: Mobilecasting or Mobilecast is a podcast file that can be transmitted to a user via cell phone. The added convenience of portability is quickly gaining popularity as more and more people have begun to use their cell phones as portable audio players. These portable podcasts are downloaded from a PC to a portable device or it can be transmitted over-the-air. Like Voicecasting, Mobilecasting refers to downloading and listening to podcasts on cellphones. When we compare this with voicecasting where the user dials a number to get the podcast, in Mobilecasting, the users subscribes to the podcast feed and automatically gets the contents on their phone without making a separate request. For some, creating/recording podcasts using a mobile phone also falls under the mobilecasts umbrella. ***GCast*** is one such service that allows users record their podcast via a toll-free call from any phone.

13. Skypecasting: Skype is a software application that allows users to make voice calls over the Internet. Skypecasting means recording your Skype conversations, conference calls and interviews for inserting in podcasts. The person who does the recording is known as a SkypeCaster while the recorded audio is called a SkypeCast. It is version of podcasting, a kind of real time blogging event with audio. Skypecasting is live, moderated conversations allowing groups of up to 100 people from anywhere in the world to talk to one another. In a Skypecast, people can discuss any topic of shared interest and give their own views about that. Skypecasts are moderated by the 'host' who can mute, eject or pass the virtual microphone to participants when they wish to speak. To host or participate in a Skypecast, user must have a Skype account, but the cost is completely free. Non-Skype users can participate only through a Skype user who has a SkypeIn number.

14. VoiceCasting : Voice casting is a vital pre-production process for selecting the voice talent for radio and television commercials, documentary and corporate narrations, audio books and online tutorials. It involves a series of auditions in front of a producer/director. VoiceCasting is rarely used on websites for audio messages about a person or product. VoiceCasting is sometimes referred as Phonecasting.

CONCLUSION

Web Technology has changed the way to broadcast/ disseminate the information. There are many choices available over the web to broadcast the digital contents. The popular broadcasting medias covered here are very useful for E-learning, E-tutorials, Web-based learning, Online learning, Distance learning and Instructional programmes etc. Most of these tools are Open Source and easy to learn and use, so the library professionals can also create various novel information dissemination services by customizing for utilising the controlling facilities available in these packages. Thus these tools may provide upper hand to the library professionals to disseminate and share information in easy, expeditious and innovative way. Librarians can implement them for enriching their services, especially in present scenario when the users tend to remain away from the libraries due to excessive use of Internet and other e-resources.

REFERENCES

1. Bowers, Andy., 15th May 2006. “Today’s Papers” on Your iPod. *Slate.* Available at: *http://www.slate.com/id/2141802/*
2. *http://textcasts.visit-rimini.com/*
3. Oud, Joanne., 2009. Guidelines for effective online instruction using multimedia screencasts. *Reference Services Review,* 37 (2), pp. 164-177. Available at: *http://wlu.openrepository.com/wlu/bitstream/10543/117100/1/Oudscreencast_article.pdf*
4. Kadel, Robert ., 2006. Coursecasting: The Wave of the Future?. *Learning & Leading with Technology,* 33 (5) pp.48-49. Available at *http://www.eric.ed.gov/PDFS/EJ728949.pdf*
5. Manya Mohan. 2009. Available at: *http://slideshare.zendesk.com/entries/57601-what-is-slidecasting*
6. *http://www.encyclo.co.uk/search.php*
7. *http://www.quickstartvoip.com/articles/new-skype-release-2-5.html*

5

DELNET : A Functional Resource-sharing Library Network in South Asia

Dr. Sangeeta Kaul

Network Manager, DELNET-Developing Library Network

INTRODUCTION

India, the largest democracy in the world with an estimated population of 114 millions has more than 1,00,000 libraries comprising academic libraries, public libraries, special libraries and libraries attached to the research and development institutions, government departments and ministries, etc. There is no denying the fact ICT has brought a paradigm change in the functionality of the libraries in the country but this technological change pattern is not seen uniformly across the wide-section of the libraries in the country. On one hand the country is proud to have the most sophisticated libraries with ISO certifications and the implementation of modern tools and technologies, on the other hand, we do encounter the challenges of providing a better infrastructure in the form of PCs and Internet connectivity in the libraries that are still striving hard to get the necessary hardware and Internet connectivity in their libraries from their managements. The adoption of standards, retrospective conversion work, the adoption of suitable library software packages continues to remain as the major areas of concerns for the libraries and the library and information science professionals.

In such constraints and hostile conditions, DELNET has been able to establish itself as an effective, operational resource sharing library network in India. The network whose journey started as a city based library network in 1988, emerged as a major operational library network not only in India but in South Asia, connecting more than 1900 libraries in 32 States and UTs in India and seven other countries. The network is growing from strength to strength, with escalating resources of union catalogues, the wider coverage of libraries from varied disciplines, the growing number of users and the horizontal and vertical expansion in its services to its members. This paper highlights the incredible and pioneering work being done by DELNET-Developing Library Network (formerly Delhi Library Network) which is a non-governmental, non-profit making organisation with inputs from the Ministry of Communications and Information Technology, Government of India and located in its own building in the well-known academic environment of Jawaharlal Nehru University at New Delhi. I would like to reiterate that DELNET do not receive any government funding and is based on a self-sustainable model, it is considered as a role model for the library networks especially of the developing nations.

THE OBJECTIVES

The main objectives of DELNET are to promote

resource sharing among member-libraries, develop a network of libraries, collect, store and disseminate information, offer computerised services to the users and coordinate efforts for suitable collection development and for reducing unnecessary duplication wherever possible.

These objectives can only be achieved if the libraries develop their catalogues in machine-readable form using international standards. This helps DELNET to create union catalogues of the resource that are available in member-libraries. As a result each library has access to greater information and is able to exchange records with any other member-library, in the country.

THE STANDARDS

DELNET promotes the use of MARC 21 format, Library of Congress Subject Headings and Dewey Decimal Classification. DELNET offers software support for creating MARC 21 records and gives guidelines for using the requisite international standards. However, libraries that use CCF or other standards are joining DELNET and slowly upgrading their records. DELNET makes every effort to incorporate into its union catalogues all such records prepared by its member-Institutions.

DELNET MEMBERSHIP

Members Statistics in different States (as on January 12, 2011)

Andaman and	2
Andhra Pradesh	199
Arunachal Pradesh	2
Assam	8
Bihar	9

Chandigarh	5
Chhattisgarh	19
Delhi	213
Goa	6
Gujarat	54
Haryana	76
Himachal Pradesh	9
Jammu & Kashmir	14
Jharkhand	12
Karnataka	145
Kerala	60
Madhya Pradesh	71
Maharashtra	203
Manipur	4
Meghalaya	2
Mizoram	2
Nagaland	2
Odisha	52
Puducherry	9
Punjab	75
Rajasthan	98
Sikkim	5
Tamilnadu	298
Tripura	3
Uttar Pradesh	181
Uttarakhand	22
West Bengal	51
Total	**1911**

Other SAARC Countries	
Nepal	3
Pakistan	1
Sri Lanka	6
Total 10	

Outside SAARC	
Philippines	1
United Arab Emirates	3
USA	4
Oman	3
Total	11
GRAND TOTAL	**1932**

Subject-wise Breakup	
General	418
Humanities	29
Science & Technology	1296
Social Sciences	189
Total	**1932**

Types of Libraries	
Academic	1706
Government Library	37
Lib. of Diplomatic Missions/UN Agency	8
Miscellaneous/Trust	46
Public Library	7
Research/Special	128
Total	1932

DELNET DATABASE

With the high-speed telecommunication facilities existing across the country and the growth of Internet Service Providers, DELNET is finding in a better position now to let researchers, scholars and readers in the country access more than 1 crore bibliographic records with holdings data through more than 1900 libraries in the country and seven other countries. These resources are growing every day as more and more libraries join DELNET from different parts of India and as they send their records in machine-readable form for merging into the DELNET union catalogues.

The following is the breakup of the DELNET databases:

1.	Union Catalogue of Books	92,76,112
2.	Union Catalogue of Periodicals	20,235
3.	Union List of Current Periodicals	33,916
4.	Articles Database	9,12,042
5.	CD-ROM Database	11,715
6.	Union List of Video Recordings	5,000
7.	Union List of Sound Recordings	748
8.	Database of Theses and Dissertations	48,621
	Total	1,03,08,389

Union Catalogue of Books

DELNET maintains an online union-catalogue of books available with its Member-Libraries. This union catalogue is continuously updated and is growing in size. The information can be retrieved by title, author, subject descriptors, series, date of publication, place and publisher, corporate body, location code and ISBN. It has about 93 lakh bibliographic records in it. The request for interlibrary loan can be placed online through the Web.

Union List of Current Periodicals

DELNET has created union list of current periodicals. It covers periodicals in all subjects including Science and Technology, Social Sciences and Humanities. This database is available online to DELNET users. It now lists 33,916 periodicals and is being updated regularly with new titles and locations.

Union Catalogue of Periodicals

DELNET maintains a union catalogue of periodicals, which, contains besides full holdings data of periodicals available in its member-libraries. At present the union catalogue contains about 20,235 records.

Database of Periodical Articles

The database has articles on various subjects which can be searched under the title, author, compiler, name of the periodical, subject descriptors, date of publication, ISSN and location. The database is being extensively used by the researchers and scholars. At present the database contains about 9 lakh records.

Union List of CD-ROMs

The CD-ROMs available with the member-libraries have been compiled in this union list. The database has about 11,715 records.

Union List of Video Recordings

The union list of video cassettes is available in member-libraries. The database has about 5,000 records.

Union List of Sound Recordings

This union list contains about 748 audio cassettes available in member-libraries.

Database of Theses and Dissertations

The database of theses and dissertations available with the member libraries of DELNET conducting research, including the Universities contains 48,621 records.

National Bibliographic Database

DELNET undertook the compilation of the National Bibliographic Database with the support of the Department of Culture, Government of India in 1998 as a Pilot Project. 50,000 records of books: 20,000 in English, 15,000 in Tamil and 15,000 in Punjabi were created at the Punjabi University, Patiala and International Institute of Tamil Studies, Chennai. Another 50,000 records were created at Andhra University Library, Visakhapatnam and Asiatic Society of Bombay, Mumbai in English, Telugu, Marathi and Sanskrit.

Important Links

DELNET offers links to Engineering & Technology E-Journals : Table of Contents, Cambridge Dictionaries Online, GISTNIC Databases, ENVIS : Environmental Information System, US Patents : Full Text, Networked Digital Library of Theses and Dissertations, MEDLINE & Other Database of NLM, SARAI : South Asia Resource Access on the INTERNET, and Library of Congress Catalogues.

ILL/DOCUMENT DELIVERY SERVICE

Inter Library Loan/Document Delivery Division of DELNET responds to ILL requests for books and DDS for periodical articles by providing books on loan as well as to arrange the journal articles. This service is provided for specially identified items by users while searching the databases online. The service is being offered to promote resource sharing at the national and international levels. DELNET has published ILL Guidelines for this purpose.

Member-Institutions make use of this service on the payment of ILL-Online fee of Rs. 4,000 per year to DELNET besides photocopying and postal/courier charges.

AICTE-DELNET MOU

Under the AICTE-DELNET MOU, it is considered that the modernization and networking of libraries of affiliated institutions of AICTE is important. It helps the students and staff to get access to the best available resources on the topics of their study. It introduces them to the latest technological inputs for modernising their libraries and in reducing expenditures on buying publications. DELNET has been regularly networking the libraries of the affiliated institutes of AICTE. From January 2010 all AICTE approved and accredited institutions are required to pay all requisite fees themselves.

DIGITAL LIBRARY SOLUTIONS

DELNET also undertakes the creation of digital libraries. Institutions can apply to DELNET for project details.

CONSULTANCY SERVICES

DELNET provides consultancy services to institutions for a variety of activities including modernization / automation of libraries.

SOFTWARE

In order to modernize and network libraries, DELNET provides free DELPLUS - the Library Management Software to member-libraries. It conforms to international standards. DELPLUS is designed to cater to the needs of various types of small and medium size libraries with a collection of books up to 1,00,000.

DELNET also offers support in the use of Koha - An Open-Source Library Management Software.

TRAINING

DELNET arranges training programmes, lecturers, workshops and the National Convention on Knowledge, Library and Information Networking (NACLIN) every year. NACLIN 2011 will be held from Nov 15-17, 2011 at Visva Bharati, Santiniketan. Special concessions are provided to the professionals of member-institutions for participation in these programmes.

HOW TO JOIN DELNET

Any Institution/Library interested in using DELNET resources for research and reference, and having any number of books in its library can join as an institutional member of DELNET.

Application Form

The membership and MOU forms are available at the following Web Address:

http://www.delnet.nic.in/membership-form.htm

Libraries interested in joining DELNET should apply on a prescribed form. The fees for membership are kept very low. At present the rates are as follows:

Membership Rates

INDIA and Other SAARC Countries

Admission Fee (one-time)	Rs.5,000/-
Institutional Membership Fee	Rs.7,500/- per annum

Non-SAARC Countries

Admission Fee (one-time)	US$100/-

Institutional Membership Fee US$500/- per annum

ILL Charges (Optional)

ILL Online Charges (for members in Delhi). Rs.4,000/- per year. Actual photocopying charges, if any, and courier/postal charges for documents, books procured from outside Delhi including NCR will be extra.

ILL Online charges (for members outside Delhi) Rs.4,000/- per year. Actual photocopying charges and courier charges will be extra.

AGENDA FOR THE FUTURE

DELNET is wanting to undertake the following tasks/projects in the days to come:

1. DELNET intends to network both libraries and knowledge in the integrated network model. While on one hand the National Knowledge Commission of the Government of India has identified DELNET as one of the major library network which will network more than 25,000 libraries in the near future in India, on the other, DELNET is supporting the establishment of Knowledge Centres and tries to create Knowledge which will be of interest to the common man. We hope that through these two networking channels, DELNET will be able to contribute a great deal not only to the modernization and networking of Libraries but also to the emerging knowledge society.
2. DELNET is keen to open shortly the State Centres in different parts of India and also the Regional Centres in order to provide training to the library professionals, promote the usage of network resources and also to help the local libraries in the development of the digital content.

3. DELNET is wanting that more libraries especially specializing in South Asian studies from different parts of the World should become a part of the network and utilize the services and resources created for their researchers and scholars at much affordable cost.

6

The Academic Libraries of Future

Dr. R.D. Mehla
Chief Librarian, JLN Library,
Kurukshetra University, Kurukshetra, Haryana, India

INTRODUCTION

Academic library Serves institutions of higher learning such as colleges & university. Vision of academic/research libraries is to ensure the survival of values libraries represent for their future existence. Technological developments have important implications for libraries

Challenges

- Budget cut.
- Low Recognition.
- Academic libraries in India have strangely been neglected.
- Inadequate funding.
- Inadequate human and material resources.

- Rapid changes in Higher Educational system in India.

Envision of Technological Changes

- Visual infra structure of video displaying walls.
- Situation Room Theaters.
- Learning Cafeterias.
- Learning with Cybrarians.
- Librarian- Technologists.

Envision of Changes in Library Functions

- Range of services to be offered (face to face and at a distance) to package e-documents primarily generated by libraries rather than by commercial publishers.
- SDI and alert system linked to a students' course management account and supported by virtual reference will highlight.
- Customization and personalization are seen as key value added contributions.
- Access to pre-prints, software, list serve archives, website and other currently overlooked resources will become common place and necessary
- Open Access Archives
- "Self Service" information finding will not push the profession aside.
- People will continue to come to Librarians because they lack the time and skills to efficiently do the job themselves.

Collection Development

- Bulk collections in academic libraries in India are in print format

- The print format convenient to most users because they are easy to use/access convenient mode of information -can be moved around.
- Electronic resources have a richer mixture of content a very good information searching/retrieval abilities.
- Future academic libraries should have majority of holding in electronic with backup files.
- Need to review/update collection development polices/procedures to reflect changing dynamics.

Change in Library Services

- Future academic library must have clear/precise objectives.
  - About people it serves
  - Those who server them
- Should be able to identity target group and offer commensurate services.
- Shift from print to digital information to provide end-users with seamless connection to internet-based services.
- Training of users to be the most important services of a user-oriented library.

Information Literacy (IL)

- Information literacy important in contemporary environment of rapid technological change and proliferating information resources.
- Individuals faced with diverse, abundant information choices.
- IL assists academic library users to evaluate/make effective use of information.

- IL is made a compulsory module for first year students.

The New Academic Librarian

- Digital Initiatives
- Flexible Experts/Specialists
- Skilled Technologists
- Vision of future library incomplete if librarians do not have vision of what their libraries should be.
- Knowledge/experience, characteristics/ image will decide the future of the library.
- The academic librarian of the future must be a researcher, counselor, planner, manager, assessor, team member, problem-solver and computer-printer repairman.
- The academic librarian of the future is expected to be multi-skilled-must have a very good interpersonal and communication skills, language proficiency, team-working skills, user friendliness and customer oriented.

Flexible Experts/Specialists

- Subject librarian-an-expert in the bibliographical organization of a field of knowledge, and who utilizes this expertise to provide complex and needed services to a clientele.
- Role of subject specialist include.
- Collection development - skilled assistance in maximizing use collection bibliographical control of the collection.
- Acquisition of library materials could be done by a team of subject librarians to ensure a balanced collection.

CONCLUSION

Future academic libraries to move away from the old ways of services delivery to technological trends in organizing/delivering information. Understand how and why libraries and library use are changing if they are to be position themselves effectively.

RECOMMENDATIONS

- Future academic librarian be conversant with the current problems facing academic and research libraries.
- Growth of ICTs - the advent of e-resources and the Internet in general have changed the way academic libraries operate today.
- The need to have the requisite human and material resources for digitization.
  - Strategies to adopted to address.
  - declining library budget.
  - growing numbers of academic publications.
  - changes in teaching and learning methods.
  - Rapid growth of ICT's.
- Academic/research institutions aim at setting up institutional repositories and build digital collections.
- Fundamental changes in the management's perception of academic and research institutions towards their libraries.

7

Role of Library and Information Professionals in Digital Era

Manish Kumar

Assistant Professor, Department of Library and Information Science, University of Delhi, Delhi, India.

ABSTRACT

This paper clearly reflects the changing role of library and information professionals in the digital era. The technology has aptly revolutionized the whole world and the impact is very significant in the library and information sector. To match the information needs of the users the library and library professionals have to change their skills, knowledge and services.

Keywords : Library, Library Professionals, Web 2.0, Digital library, Information Librarianship, Information Officer, Information literacy.

INTRODUCTION

In today's environment, knowledge is in transition mode from repositories to open access and print to digital. Libraries have been significantly transformed with the advent of information and communication technology (ICT), Internet and the ability to provide resources to people to their own homes or work places. The unimaginable developments in the information environment such as improved accessibility, interoperability and open access to educational materials has on one side facilitated the nature, role and services but on the other side pose a serious challenge use technology and provide efficient and effective services to meet the users information needs. In the present technological/Internet era the professionals have to change themselves, as the **information** profession is being changed. Now **information** specialists have to work as e-**information** providers in which various **professional** groups are expected to map strategies that lead to produce, manage, maintain and service the **information.**

CURRENT TRENDS IN LIBRARIANSHIP

It is very much important that we should discuss first the new role of librarians and information professionals in the digital age. These current trends somehow or rather will have a bearing in shaping librarians and information professionals in the new era. They are summarized as follows (Hashim and Mokhtar, 2005):

- A vision towards information and knowledge rich society;
- Library functions in information and knowledge-based society;
- Knowledge-based economy-information and knowledge as drivers to boost the economy;

- Information management recognized as an important discipline;
- Information recognized as commodity (information brokerage, information entrepreneurship, fee-based information);
- Information recognized as power/strength/weapon;
- Information strongly link to decision-making, strategic management, competitive advantage, innovation, R&D;
- Knowledge Management-leveraging organization;
- Globalisation of information;
- Integrated and widespread ICT application;
- Mushrooming of information systems - need for Information System Management (ISM);
- Growth of electronic / Internet resources;
- Role of digital/electronic/virtual library;
- Librarian is designated as cyber librarians;
- Librarians expanded and changes in digital environment;
- New breeds of information professionals: CIO, CKO, Information consultants and analysts;
- Competency - based assessment/training;
- Leadership skills;
- Access role replace custodial role;
- Customer-focused/customer-centered, user oriented approach in provision of services;
- Strategic alliances, partnership and collaborations;
- Librarians need new management knowledge and skills;

- Specialized knowledge and skills in library and information management;
- Double degree (major-minor concept);
- Trend to develop digital contents to facilitate access to information;
- Revamping of curriculum - redesign curriculum to accommodate changes and new trends.

ROLE OF LIS PROFESSIONALS

Library plays an important role in supplementing classroom teaching and it is the librarians who disseminate the precise information contained in the documents to its users in efficient and effective manner. With the advancements of electronic technology, it becomes very difficult for an individual to get the required information without wasting their time. It's the information managers, who have to make the required information available to the individual without wasting his/her time. The information professionals have to keep pace with the latest developments that are taking place due to the advancement of technology. It is not possible that the existing information professional to go to library schools however, training can be arranged for them to have an bird's eye view about the developments that are taking place. The changes taking place in the corporate environment are challenging the librarians to reorient his/her skill to provide information solutions, not just information or information sources. Information professionals have to take into consideration the following aspects before collecting information for the end product, which they have to offer:

- It must be according to needs and requirements of its users;
- It must be equipped with powerful, easy to use,

intelligent search engines;

- It must have attractive user interface;
- It must be reasonably priced;
- It must allow access from, and delivery to the users' workstation;

In the present scenario, the library and information professionals have to keep in mind the following points to keep pace with the modern trends, if they want to survive:

- Continuous updating;
- Developing strong professional teams in their respective libraries;
- Arranging continuous education and training programs for users and staff;
- Accept the challenges being imposed due to advancement of technology;
- Arrange lectures/training programs from time to time (Gupta, Singh and Negi, 2005);
- Be alert and Innovative;
- Willing to learn;
- Identify specific areas in which technology can advance the institution in fulfilling its mission;
- Enable users to interact with knowledge resources;
- Sound communication skills;
- Provide quality services;
- Expertise in the use of innovative emerging technologies to design and develop web-based applications, programmes and services;
- Assist users to locate, access, store and transform

electronic information resources, services and instructions across multiple applications, databases, networks, platforms and systems through an academic library's information commons;

- Having knowledge of designing, developing, launching and maintaining of digital content management and assess, evaluate, recommend and test various methodologies, policies, and standards for utilizing computer software in the process of creating and preserving digital process of creating and preserving digital collections and resources.
- Assess, understand, think and adopt changes fit to the requirements rather become blind follower of versatile technological developments (Li 208).

DISSEMINATOR OF INFORMATION LITERACY

ALA defined information literacy is " recognizing when information is needed, and having the ability to locate, evaluate and use effectively this needed information."(wikipedia 2009). In 2003, ALA evolved this definition and set information literacy standards for student learning, strives that it is essential for higher education institutions, students and staff be provided with opportunities to learn not only how to access information sources but also how to evaluate, manage and use them effectively. Information literary forms the basis for life long learning and enables learners to master content and extent their investigations to become more self- directed, thus assuming greater control over their own learning. This leads information literate individuals to address:

- Assess the extent of information needed;
- Access the desired information effectively and efficiently;

- Use information effectively;
- Evaluate information and its resources critically; and
- Incorporate selected information into their knowledge base (Nyamboga 233).

The academic library has to provide information literacy services to introduce known and unknown information sources to users by discharging its prime function of service oriented knowledge centre.

STAFF RESPONSIBILITY

The behaviour, role, skills and services of staff member need to be changed in today's electronic environment. The library staff should have strong technical skills and an ability to identify specific areas in which technology can advance the institution in fulfilling its academic mission. They should understand the user information needs, work effectively in partnership with faculty members to enhance teaching and research activities, willing to learn new skills for efficient and effective services and work not only for the sake of duty but also for true service (ALA 2009). Open access publishing and institutional repositories are new paradigms of electronic environment and information professionals not only need to respond to changing user expectations and relationship between stakeholders in scholarly publishing, they are also required to work in different partnership models with other academic services and other professional groups, which can take them far beyond the traditional concept of libraries, creating new models of holistic student support, learning environments and teaching and research collaborations (Griffiths and Craven 197). Thus, staff should observe the following:

- Be alert, innovative and creative;
- Willing to learn and adopt to environment;

- Identify specific areas in which technology can advance the institution in fulfilling its academic mission;
- Enable users to interact with knowledge resources;
- Sound communication skills; and
- Provide quality services.(Nyamboga 233)

ROLE OF LIBRARIAN

In addition to general qualification and requirements, a commitment to excellent user- centered services, effective oral and written communications, as well as team collaborator must also possess additional capabilities, experience, knowledge and skills such as:

1. Expert in the use of innovative emerging technologies to design and develop web- based applications, programmes and services.
2. Having knowledge of designing, developing, launching and maintaining of digital content management and assess, evaluate, recommend and test various methodologies, policies, and standards for utilizing computer software in the process of creating and preserving digital collections and resources
3. As information management consultants, librarians can help network users build and maintain personal information systems, which provide access to the subset of networked information sources relevant to each user's work.
4. As custodians of information, librarians are facing apparent challenges to their role, as physical resources migrate into electronic form and on-demand electronic delivery becomes more common. The ephemeral nature of much electronic materials (such as

newsgroups) does, however create a need to identify and where appropriate, archive authoritative versions of electronic information.

5. As information providers, librarians can make available much more widely collections which previously can be used only within a single physical library location. A wide range of publications and access formats can be accommodated, from remote login catalogues and indexes, to provision of electronic copies of entire collection or works, in print or other formats.
6. As change agents, library staff can lobby managers and governments as appropriate, for network access for themselves and their users.
7. As custodians of public library facilities, information professionals can provide workstations, network gateways, printers and software that may not be otherwise available to the public.
8. Assess, understand, think and adopt changes fit to the requirements rather become blind follower of versatile technological developments(Li 179-81).

CONCLUSION

The role of library professionals has changed in the digital era. It is, therefore pertinent on the part of professionals to acquire new skills required for developing and managing the digital libraries. The library and information professionals are required to acquire such knowledge and skills as the library is one of the highly IT influenced service profession. The empowerment of library and information professionals with IT skills is aimed at providing services that are expected by the users in the new electronic environment.

REFERENCES

ALA. Changing roles. accessed on 12.06.2009. http://www.ala.org./ala/mgrps/divs/acrl/issues/future/changing roles.cfm

Griffiths, J R and Craven, J, ed. 2008. Access, delivery, performance: the future of libraries without walls. Facet Publishing, London.

Gupta, Sanjay., Singh, Birmohan and Negi, Anukampa Digital Libraries and changing role of Information Managers. 2005. Retrieved from http://library.igcar.gov.in/readit-2005/conpro/lgw/s5-2.pdf.

Hashim, Laili bin, and Mokhtar, Wan Nor Haliza Wan, 2005. Trends and Issues in Preparing New Librarians and Information Professional. Universiti Teknologi MARA (UITM). Malaysia. MARA University of Technology.

Li, LiLi, 2009. Emerging technologies for academic libraries in the digital age. England, Chandos Publishing.

Nyamboga, C M, 2004. Information skills and information literacy in Indian university libraries. Program: electronic library and information systems. 38.4 (2004): 233

Wikipedia. Information literacy. accessed on 07.06.2009.http://en.wikipedia.org/wiki/Information_Literacy

8

Essential in Planning Digital Library

Sandhya Aggarwal
Librarian, M.M.P.G.College, Fatehabad
Haryana - 125050

ABSTRACT

Library is a store house of knowledge and with the advent of Information Technology, information explosion, whole concept of library has been changed. Digital library is an indispensable need in today's world. In the digital world of information, stress should be on these things: awareness of information, awareness of technology and awareness of needs.

INTRODUCTION

Rapid advances in information processing, storage and communication technology have changed the role of libraries in dissemination of information service to their users. As a result, libraries are facing new challenges, new competitors, new demands, new expectations and variety of information Services from users needs.

Process of Digitization

Librarians are required to select, acquire, organize, make accessible and preserve digital collection. First of all, Archival material must be converted into electronic form by Optical Character Recognition (OCR) using Readiris12 or Omni page Software etc. It is used to convert paper books and images in to electronic form. Manually by scanning a document, an image file created as in Figure 1 (Source: www.irislink.com/readiris)

Fig. 1. Scanning of Paper or Document

However, using special software converts them into a text or word processor file so that editing or change is possible in the file as shown in Figure 2 and 3

Fig. 2. Process by Software

Fig. 3. Paper is ready for editing

Now create desktop folders to organize scanned files. When editing is completed, you have e-book or digital collection on your desktop.

Digital Library Architecture

The extent of utilization of a digital library material depends completely on the existence of the comprehensive metadata to give an efficient and accurate view of content. A digital library system may consist of four layers as shown in figure 4.

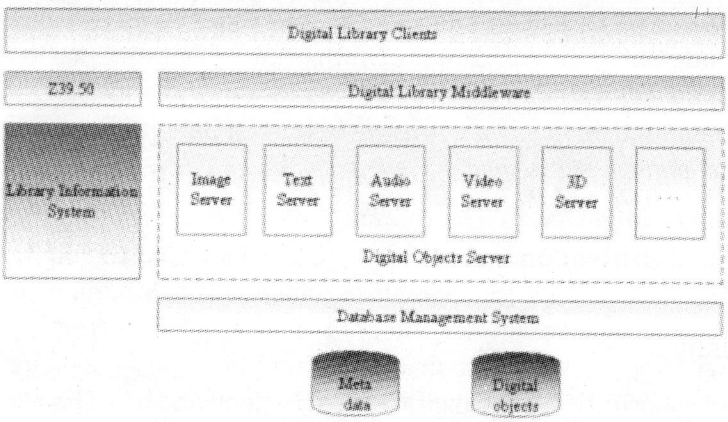

Fig. 4. Digital Library Architecture

(Source: Bogen and others)

Digital objects and the related metadata information are stored in a database. Digital objects server handles all requests for this DBMS concerning digital objects depending on the media type, a request is handled by an image server, a text server, an audio server, a video server or server for other digitized objects respectively. In the mid there is a layer called Digital Library Middleware. It is defined as the glue that keeps networks and applications together, it is also called repository. It includes toolkits for clients. The Digital Library Clients requesting, any information send requests through user interface. Z39.50 is an interface that provides access to conventional library information and satisfies user's query.

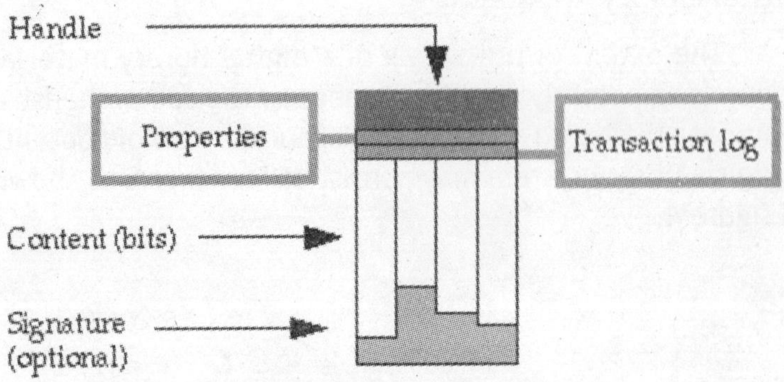

Fig. 5. Parts of a digital object
(Source: www.cnri.reston.va.us/.../object.html)

Information is stored as Digital Objects, in the digital library. It has the following components as shown in Figure 5. These types of digital objects are very different from the digital objects that are made available from other sources, not repositories. Each digital object is identified by its handle and contains many types of contents i.e. text, graphics, images, videos, audios etc. All the contents and metadata are stored in repository.

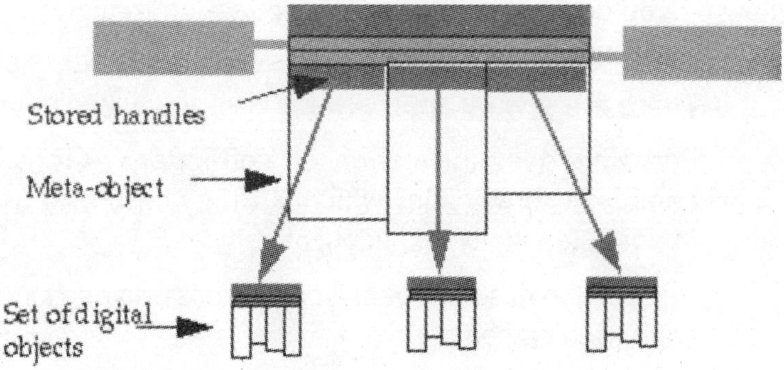

Fig. 6. A digital object used as a catalog record (Source: www.dlib.org/dlib/july95/07/arms.html)

Issues involved in Digital Libraries

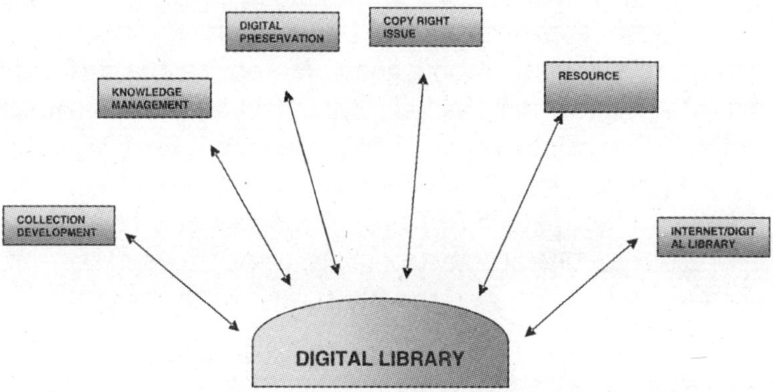

Fig. 7

COLLECTION DEVELOPMENT

The success of a digital library depends largely on the nature, content and quality of its digital collections. Information required for collection includes various resources such as electronic journals, books, CD- ROM databases etc. Expensiveness and time constraint are in the digitization obstacles. To resolve these two issues some part of knowledge should be digitized. Now the question arises how do you decide what parts of a collection to digitize of any institution?

There are several approaches:

- Retrospective Conversion of collections - it is a complete conversion, which is time consuming and impossible legally and economically.
- Digitization of some special collections or a portion of collection can be digitized.
- Highly used material- According to demands of the resources.
- An adhoc approach - Digitize the stored material on request/demand.

These approaches can be collectively helpful to complete the institution's goals. Moreover, the different digital storage formats include Hyper Text Mark- up Language (HTML), Extensible Mark up Language (XML), Real Page Plug in, Adobe Acrobat Reader, Image Formats and Portable Document Formats (PDF) etc. To access and read these converted documents electronically, respective software are requested depending on the file format of the resources.

KNOWLEDGE MANAGEMENT

Knowledge Management is to identify, capture and provide a single point/click access to knowledge contained in multiple data stores both within and outside the organization. The key to knowledge management is how the knowledge capturing process work is done by the organizations. Two different types of information are necessary to accomplish this task: Explicit and Implicit. Explicit Information is packaged, easily codified, transferable and communicable while Implicit Information is personal, context specific, difficult to formalize and hard to communicate and transferable. Combining these two types of information provides the perceived value of knowledge management, so that the right knowledge is available to the right person at the right time.

DIGITAL PRESERVATION

In the preservation of digital material, the real issue is technical obsolescence. Technical obsolescence in the digital age is like the deterioration of paper in the paper age. Technology changes very fast e.g. Floppy disks were replaced by CDs and these are being replaced by DVDs for future use. For the preservation of digital information for future use, you have to migrating from one hardware and software media to another but during this migration process, loss/distortion of information is possible. Had we not emphasized on preservation issue, future generation would look at our time as a digital Dark Age - A time when, the records of knowledge went missing.

COPY RIGHT ISSUES

Copy right is one of the most important types of intellectual property rights. Copy right in digital environment has raised numerous legal issues and practical problems that concern the library managers, information scientists, authors, publishers and information users. The importance of copyright has grown enormously in recent times due to revolutionary developments in information publishing and accessibility especially online through internet. Thus protection of copyright has become much more complex and serious in digital environment.

METADATA

Metadata is the data that describes the contents and attributes of any particular item in a digital library. Metadata is important in digital libraries due to its resource discovery feature. There are formal library standards for metadata, namely AACR*, Dublin Core etc. The success or failure of any digital library depends on exhaustiveness of its metadata. Creating metadata is very time consuming, laborious to create and requires specially trained personnel. None use of common metadata standards is a barrier to information access and use in a digital library.

DIFFERENCE BETWEEN DIGITAL LIBRARY AND INTERNET

Many people call the huge collection on Internet as a digital library because they can find information there. The Internet collection is not designed to support the organized publications and retrieval of information as in a library is. Therefore, Internet is not a digital library.

Locating information on the Internet remains highly inefficient compared to traditional library sources. Need to learn to locate new information on the web which is more difficult than in a traditional library. In the past, the very fact that a book or a journal was held by a library represented a conscious set of decisions about the validity of the information. This is not necessarily true for information found on the web.

CONCLUSION

As with continuous technical developments in the world over the years, libraries have been facing the problems to walk with the need of the hour. Several national/ international schemes, projects and many digital library have been created for exploring key issues and overcome these problems in planning digital libraries. Investment in digitization is more difficult until technical and legal constraints are not overcome first.

Conscious selection of material to be digitized is an important step because digitization is a time consuming and costly work. Further a definite process of digitization and creating metadata should be planned.

REFERENCES

Arms, W.Y., 1995. Key concepts in the architecture of the digital library. *D-Lib Magazine www.dlib.org/dlib/july95/07arms.html* (accessed on 02nd February 2011)

Arms, William Y., Blanchi, christophe and Overly, Edward A., 1997.An architecture for information in digital libraries. *D-Lib Magazine http://www.dlib.org/dlib/february97/cnri/02arms1.html* (accessed on 01st February 2011)

Bogen and others, Requirements and architectures for administration and maintenance of digital object libraries. *Paper Museums and the Web 2001 http://www.archimuge.com/mw2001/papers/bogen/bogenfig2.html* (accessed on 02nd February 2011)

Cleveland, gary, 1998. *Digital libraries: definitions, issues and challenges.* mhtml:file://J:\digital1\digita.mht (accessed on 09th June 2010)

Ghosh, Maitrayee. Knowledge management in the digital age: challenges and opportunities in India (accessed on 09th June 2010)

Kotler, Philip, 1995. *Marketing for nonprofit organization.* 2nd ed, Ess Ess Publication, New Delhi

Lynch, C.A., 1997. Searching the internet. *Scientific American*, pp 52-56 *http://www.sciam.com/0397issue/0397lynch.html* Wikipaedia. Digital Library mhtml:file://F:\digital%201\digit.mht (accessed on 21st November 2010)

www.irislink.com/readiris

9

E-Learning: Supplementary Tool of Education

Subhash Deshmukh
University Librarian, UIRC,
Guru Gobind Singh Indraprastha University,
Delhi-110403

ABSTRACT

In the present scenario, there has occurred a paradigm shift in education and learning. Education which got influenced by ICT, has given rise to a new concept of e-learning, a concept that was originated in the western countries, but now going to become a part of daily work culture of under-developed countries. E-learning, which is fully technology dependent, is moving at a rapid pace, and to remain a part of drama, it is a need of an hour, that we must think towards it seriously and do something good to implement it. No doubt, there are projects and efforts, that are going on in our country, but all are at its infancy stage. For knitting the fabric of e-learning and to make it our culture and reality, planning at various levels, drafting of policies and principles, designing a full-proof strategy are required and this article is a step towards this. It is easy to say few words, regarding e-learning, but really difficult to administer and have support for e-learning.

The whole process of higher education has become warped, disoriented and dysfunctional and to improve the organizational efficiency and to maintain the standards, integration of IT in higher education i.e. e-learning is needed. Efforts at national level by some of the universities and institutes of national importance, to make e-learning, a common approach is on the way and discussed at large in this article.

In any educational institute, libraries are regarded as a learning resource centre, so there is a great hope and expectation from libraries and library professionals for the successful implementation of e-learning. Libraries, which are now-a-days technology driven and always a hub of resources is going to play a major role in implementing e-learning and without the elbow support of library professionals, it is very difficult to make the concept, a success. This in turn, brings new challenges and opportunities for libraries and library professionals, what are those challenges and opportunities is a part of this article.

Keywords: E-learning, Virtual learning environment, Open courseware, Learning management system, Video lectures, Web portal, E-referencing, E-content, Integrated learning system, Virtual reference desks.

INTRODUCTION

Knowledge-based economics is considered the driving engines in today's global market. Technological innovation plays a central role in achieving technological progress and economic growth. Education, life-long learning, knowledge and skills upgrading are the fuel of the knowledge based economy. Information and communication Technology (ICT) enables developing countries a chance to enjoy economic growth quickly.

Recent development in the field of information and communication technology, the sharp growth in higher education institutions, and the new delivery mode of education made tremendous impact on higher education. The classical teacher centric model can be modified to the learner-centric model using ICT. Instructors become supervisors-facilitators and learners become more self-dependent, capable of finding needed information and accessing suitable knowledge. This will lead to a true life-long education.

The new education needs urge for a renewal and an improvement of teaching methodologies, mainly concerning instruments that ICT make available for teaching activities support.

A more extensive, but technologically advanced approach, would allow an improvement of teaching, dealing with issues concerning the number of students, but also fulfilling personal and collective needs of types of students that have been changing through the years.

The present day student is in many cases, a commuter or a resident, with basic computer skills, that makes use of technologies like the internet or e-mail. Such a student has needs that we could define "of high teaching structure flexibility", as for instance:

- possibility of remotely accessing course material
- making focus discussions or submitting questions to the teacher in moments different from the compulsory "receiving hours"
- testing his/her own level of comprehension through self-evaluation to be done before official tests
- Enlist for examinations, be informed on grades, deliver projects without having to physically commute to the course premises.

From the teacher's point of view, some similar and

symmetric needs can be pointed out, like:

- possibility to distribute course material, papers, etc. with methods accessible to non-resident students, different from the traditional "entrance booth deposit"
- publish grades, collect projects and applications for examinations
- update with urgent variations and notices lesson or examination schedules
- distribute summary notes on subjects dealt with during single lessons
- interact with a high number of students on frequent issues or problems, that are usefully shared between users
- Have an overall assessment of the general level of results in courses with a very high number of students.

ICT enables students, teachers, and decision makers to obtain valuable information and to conduct time saving transactional operations related to the educational activities.

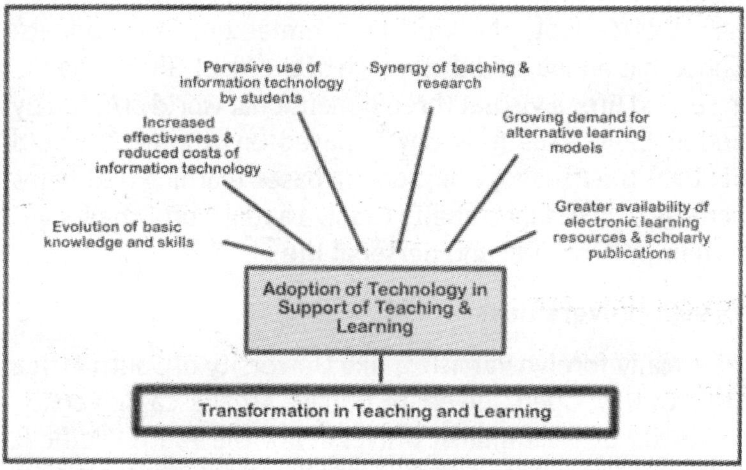

Fig. 1. Forces leading to transformation in teaching and learning

E-LEARNING AT GLOBAL ARENA

If we look the concept at international level, then we will be of the view, that it is no more a grey area for western countries, there the equation of education has changed completely and some of the foreign universities are pioneer in this field, and most ventures in third word countries are modeled around them. There is a lot to quote, but some of the current praise worthy efforts in this direction are reproduced below as:-

MIT On -line Project

Massachusetts institute of technology (MIT) on-line project called MIT open course ware, display lecture notes, previous exams and study materials offered to MIT students for anyone to access. It has all the more uploaded 1800 courses on its website. Several other universities like Yale, Peking, Harvard Law school, Tufts, UC-Irvine and Utah State University, have allowed MIT to host links to their individuals Courseware. However, no Indian universities, apart from IITs, have been invited to join this league.

U21 Global Island

U21 Global, the world's premier on line graduate school, has announced the launch of the "U21 Global Island" on second life, a virtual three dimensional world created by Linden Labs. This new participated environment would highlight the Pedagogy of problem based learning that helps increase our student's ability to solve a real world challenges in their professional and personal life.

Foreign Universities

Many foreign varsities, like University of South Africa (UNISA), U.K. Open University, Canada Athabasca University, University of West Indies, University of the South Pacific & various universities in Australia and New-Zealand and almost all commonwealth universities are offering some programmes via e-learning mode.

E-LEARNING IN INDIAN SCENARIO

The Status of E-learning in India can easily be judged, by a statement made by Karthik K.S., Founder and CEO of the Bangalore based privately held 24 x7 learning solution and according to him "One of the Principal drivers of the growth in learning management solution is e-learning. The electronic learning market is estimated to touch $ 21 billion by 2008. According to our own market Research and analysis, the e-learning market in India is over $ 200 million, most of which is carried out in house as the market matures, outsourcing of e-learning will also gain a strong hold."

E-learning is taking its deep root, slowly and slowly in every sector, whether it may be commercial or business unit, secondary education or higher education. Some of the examples from industries and education are detailed below, to have a taste of e-learning in India.

E-Learning in Corporate World (Business)

With increased competition for jobs and the trends being on continuous learning, more and more people are boosting their qualification on line, on top of this, with skilled manpower in short supply, companies in new industries domains like information technology, Pharma and retail, are relying on in-house training programmes. The numbers are mind -boggling, the complexities are huge. Adding to the complexities are new skill- sets requirements and high rates of attrition. Faced with the vexed issues, what does a company do? Simply, it implements a learning management solution. In 2005, corporate E-learning has gone up to 28% of all training delivery method (Calculated in number of training hours) as against a measly 8% in 1999.

Some of the Indian companies, where e-learning has been implemented successfully are Satyam computer services, Hyderabad and Aventis pharmaceuticals.

E-learning at Secondary Education Level

The E-learning scenario in India is still growing and is at an experimental stage, says Bhooma. "Traditional mind sets are beginning to change, with the corporate sector leading the way in embracing technology -based learning avenues. Many schools have started augmenting teacher led programmes with content rich e-learning modules. Government initiatives are not far behind either".

More than 100 schools across India and around 20 in NCR are using robotics in their class rooms to enhance creativity among students and to sharpen their brains, besides teaching them problem solving skill and teamwork.

NCERT has come up with several multimedia packages on topic in science and mathematics. Two of these multi-media CDs on chemistry and mile-stone in genetics - were already released. Six more packages are also being worked upon by NCERT. NCERT also coming up with a detailed distribution plan to make this CDs and other products like audio and video materials on topics in science and social science on a much larger scale.

Some of the private schools, where e-learning programmes are being promoted on a larger scale are:

1. Millenium School, Noida
2. Vasant Valley School, Delhi
3. Amity School , Noida
4. Apeejay School, Noida
5. Sainik School, etc.

E-learning at Higher Education Level

If the e-learning strategy is successful, new practices relating to learning and teaching will become more widely embedded in the University's activities. As we noted at the outset, "e-learning" will not remain a distinct set of activities, but will become part of the fabric of academic provision. Its implications will therefore have to be noted and taken up by the range of bodies in the University concerned with all aspects of academic life. Steering and the various finance committees will need to be apprised of the implications of e-learning developments as they effect changes in the University's culture. As "e-Learning" increasingly becomes a normal part of "learning," so responsibilities for it will diffuse into all the parts of the University engaged in its academic provision.

Gone are the days, when E-learning was assumed to be a grey area. Higher education especially universities and some of the prestigious institutes of national importance are leaving no stone unturned in inculcating and promoting e-learning. Various prominent initiatives taken by some of the Indian Institutes of Higher Education is listed below:

University of Delhi

Following are the list of activities that is in pipe line regarding e-learning at Delhi University

(i) Delhi University is planning to offer digital book and audio books available for down load by its clientele

(ii) As per the statement made by S. Majumdar, DU Librarian, the students will have excess to 150 E-references resources consisting of journals, dissertation, dictionaries, biographies and year book, irrespective of subject available on the campus

(iii) More and more DU Colleges are doing their best to modernize their facilities and offer the students a holistic learning experience, by providing WiFi connection, arranging LCD projectors during class presentation to install ACs in the community room, colleges are going the whole hog to attract the tech - savvy generation.

(iv) DU is planning to prepare and post class room lectures and other E-learning materials on to the web sites of the varsity's institute of life long learning (ILLL).

(v) To facilitates the learning process for visually challenged students and faculty members with serious vision impairment, DU is all set to launch a multi-purpose resource centre which would not only have a used collection of study material in Braille format, but also special studios to convert audio-cassettes into text message in Braille.

(vi) DU is collaborating with U.K.'s open universities (OU) for integrating technology in traditional learning and is designing the e material using OU servers and are being assessed by OU experts.

Indira Gandhi National Open University (IGNOU), New Delhi

As per Times of India News dated 16th June 2008, IGNOU has introduced the digital learning environment which would provide walk in admission, integrated multimedia courseware (personalized learning space), on-line counseling and mentoring (Web Casting and text based chatting), 24x7 learner support, assignment management system, e tutor based practical, group based online seminar and online term end examination. In this direction, following efforts by IGNOU is in pipe line and going to be operational in the days to come.

(i) Availability of Audio-Video instructional material on youtube.com

(ii) Availability of course material through web site

(iii) IGNOU has launched e-Gyankosh, online programmes and web-casting facility for gyandarshan, Edusat and Gyanvani at electronic media production centre through the tele-conference mode.

(iv) Launching of online programmes

(v) Use of video conferencing facility to participate in seminars & viva -voce.

(vi) IGNOU is also decided to introduce online examination etc.

NPTEL Project

As part of NPTEL (National Programme for Technology enhanced learning), all IITs have provided online access to their course materials, which is in two form - digitally taped classroom lectures and Web based lecture material.

Institute of Company Secretaries of India (ICSI)

ICSI has launched its e-learning portal (www.elearning.icsi.edu), which provides the 24x7 learning experience. This portal has enabled the user web based training to the subscriber by which, they can access e-books, participate in discussion and quizzes, e-mail queries & have access to online chat.

Initiative by Various B Schools

Several prominent institutions like XCRI, IIM Lucknow, IMT Ghaziabad, IIMK, IIMC IIMB, MAHE, NMIMS, NIIT, IIT-Bangalore, Symbiosis, Pune, etc. offer courses in management through the e-learning mode.

ROLES OF LIBRARIES AND LIBRARY PROFESSIONALS IN E-LEARNING

Education and libraries are the two faces of the same coin, and it is really not possible to make a separation between them. Time has changed the role, responsibility & working style of learning & teaching & so does it changed the morphology & anatomy of libraries, both are now moving towards their electronic front, and to remain on a common platform, they have to join hand in-hand.

The e-learning has influence the individual library & information workers, their services & the information profession. This has offered new opportunities & challenges for information workers in the form of acquiring new learning opportunities, developing new skills, generating new employment opportunities, acting in a new rules and responsibilities and making a balance in life and work. Involvement of library professional's workers in performing virtual activities has added to the already demanding work load of some information workers, but nevertheless, library and information professionals have responded to the challenges and often take a lead role with in their organization.

The role and responsibilities of libraries/ professionals in the new learning and teaching activities involves.

1. Providing web based learning technologies
2. Providing new services and resources to customer
3. Managing e-learning centres
4. Managing integrated learning systems
5. Create develop and maintain websites
6. Development of contents of materials for e-learning programmes

7. Design, development and delivery of e-learning programmes
8. Supporting e-learners
9. Responding to students queries via bulletin board or producing Frequently Asked Question (FAQ) list
10. E-tutoring
11. Managing and taking part in collaborative e-learning programmes or projects
12. Providing supports and helps to e-learners via e-mail, virtual reference desks, bulletin board, chat room, FAQ list etc.
13. Training students in the use of virtual learning environment

This is not a comprehensive list but a short of basic activities, require to be done, but one thing is sure that at a professional level, e-learning and teaching is changing initial and continuing professional education and training.

FREE EDUCATION WITH THE HELP OF E-LEARNING

The basic motto of e-learning is to provide universal access to education. This can not be achieved by simply saying it as such, and gamuts of activities are required to rise to this status. One such activity is to create e- content, designing and creating open courseware and providing cross archive search services.

In the wake of open access initiatives, there is an ongoing struggle to make academic work more widely available and increasing number of high quality subject specific archives are now freely available online. Various national and international organization, commission and conferences are strongly in favour of open access initiatives and they are in favour of making academic material accessible freely 24x7 x365 days.

Internet which is a hub of resources and facilitates learning has a long list of this open Courseware, and these coursewares are not restricted to a particular stream, but one can find, this courseware for every subjects. The prominent academic institution like MIT, Stanford University, IITs and IIMs in Indian scenario, are trying their best to make free availability of these open courseware. Some such types of courseware are discussed in brief below as:

Free Video Lectures. Com (http://freevideoletures.com)

The main motto of this site is to bring free education to everyone. Through this site one can access the freely available videos of the lectures on various subjects specially on anatomy and physiology, Astronomy and Aerospace, Bio-Sciences, Business and Management, Chemistry , Computer Science, Economics, Electronic, Genetic, Health Science, Law, Mathematics, Medicine, Networking, Philosophy, Physics, Psychology, Signal and Systems, Web Designing etc.

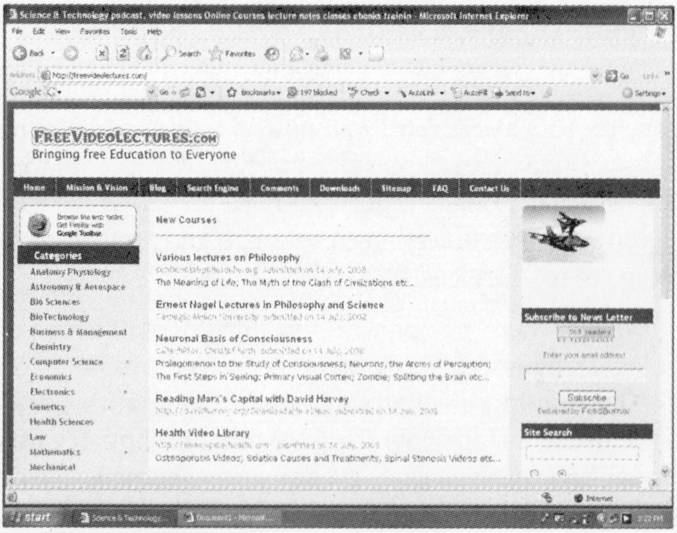

National Programme on Technology Enhance Learning (NPTEL) :- (http://nptel.iitm.ac.in)

This is a collaborative project of all IITs and IISC Bangalore and is fully supported by a grant from the Ministry of Human Resource Development, Government of India. The main objective of NPTEL programme is to enhance the quality of engineering education in the country by developing curriculum based video and web courses. There are at present 129 web courses available in engineering/science and humanities discipline. The major engineering disciplines which have been covered in this project are:-

1. Civil engineering
2. Computer Science and Engineering
3. Electrical Engineering
4. Electronic and Communication Engineering
5. Mechanical Engineering

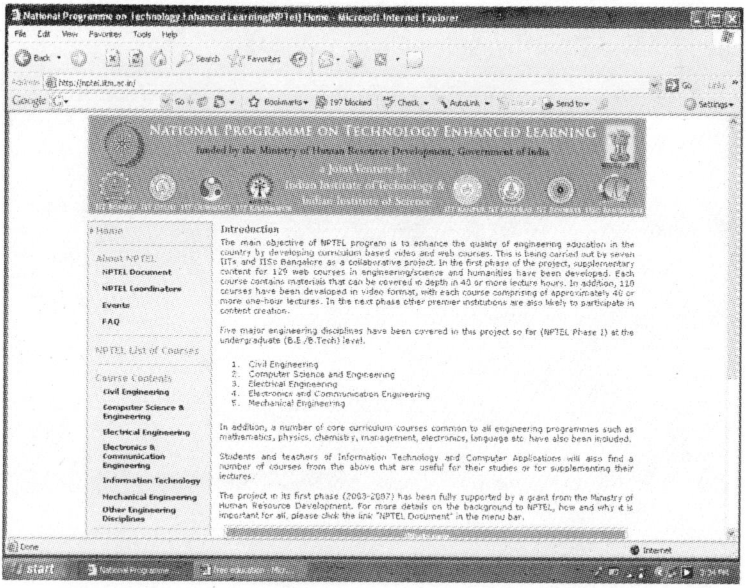

MIT Open Courseware (http://ocw.mit.edu/index.html)

It is a site, where one can access the web based publication of virtually all MITs course content. This includes audio video and translated course.

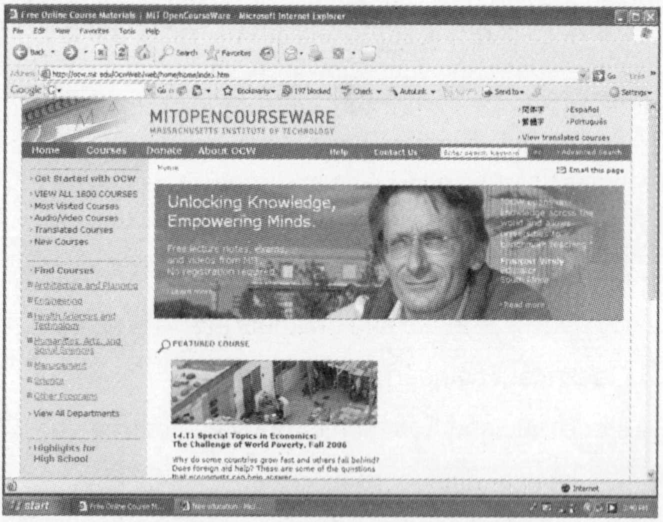

MIT WORLD (http://mitworld.mit.edu)

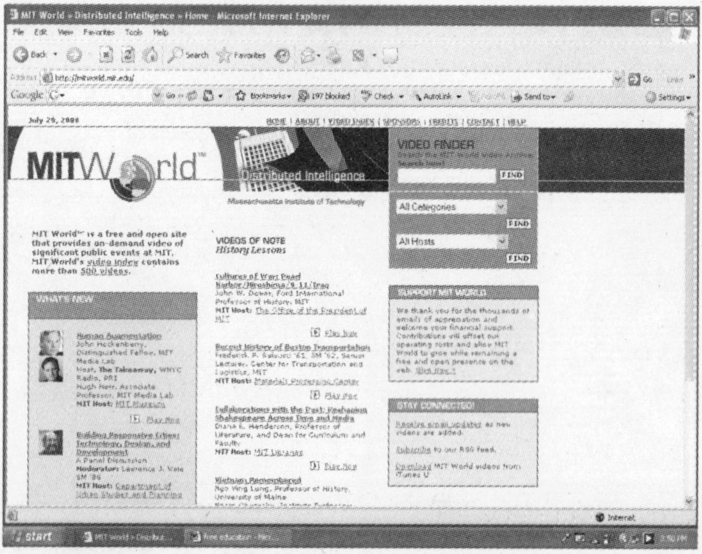

MIT world is a free, open streaming media website of the most significant public events at MIT. It features speakers and guests from across the campus and around the world; the collection dates backs to February 2001, and holds more than 500 video lectures

World Lecture Hall (WLH) (http://web.austin. utexas.edu /wlh/index.cfm)

This site contains links to course material for university level courses, which are created by faculty world wide, who are using the web to deliver course material in any language. This site contains course material in almost all the subjects and in particular courses related to Finance and Investment, Leadership and Change , Executive Education, Marketing, Insurance and Pension, Health Economics, Strategic Management, Real Estate, Law and Public Policy, Human Resources, Business Ethics, Innovation and Entrepreneurship, Operation Management, Managing Technology Etc.

WGBH Forum Network (http://wgbh.org/wgbh)

The WGBH Forum Network is an audio and video streaming website dedicated to curating and serving live and on demand lectures giving by some of the world's foremost scholar, authors, artists, scientist, policy maker and community leaders. The present day collection is over 2000 lectures and 200 curated series. The subject area covered by this site include Art and Architecture, Astronomy, Business and Economics, Dance, Education, Environment, Health , History, Law, Literature, Media , Music, Philanthropy, Philosophy, Poetry, Politics, Psychology, Religion, Science, Society and Culture, Sport, Technology, Theatre Etc.

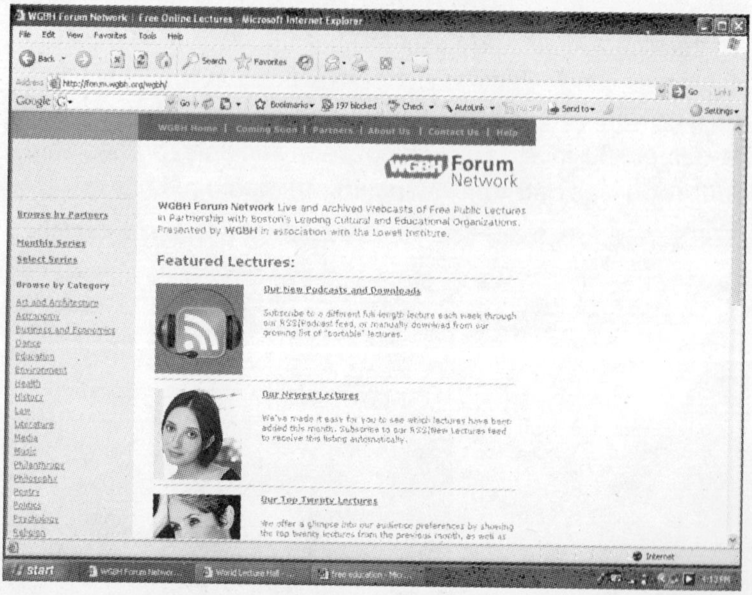

Microbiology Video Library (http://www.microbiology bytes.com/video)

This site contains hundreds of videos on almost all the topics related to microbiology. Besides this, site also provides various services like microbiology blogs, microbiology post cads, lab work, on line tutorials etc.

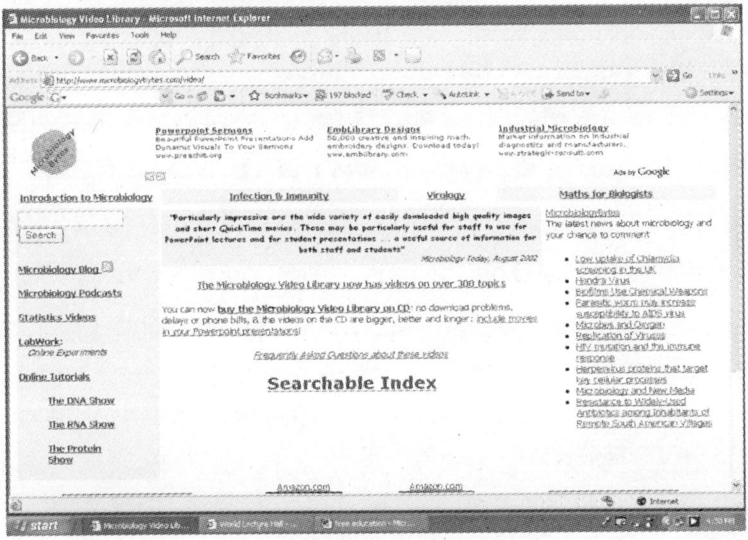

Max Animation (http://maxanim.com)

This site gives a comprehensive course material in animated form on genetics, bio-chemistry, immunology, physiology, microbiology etc.

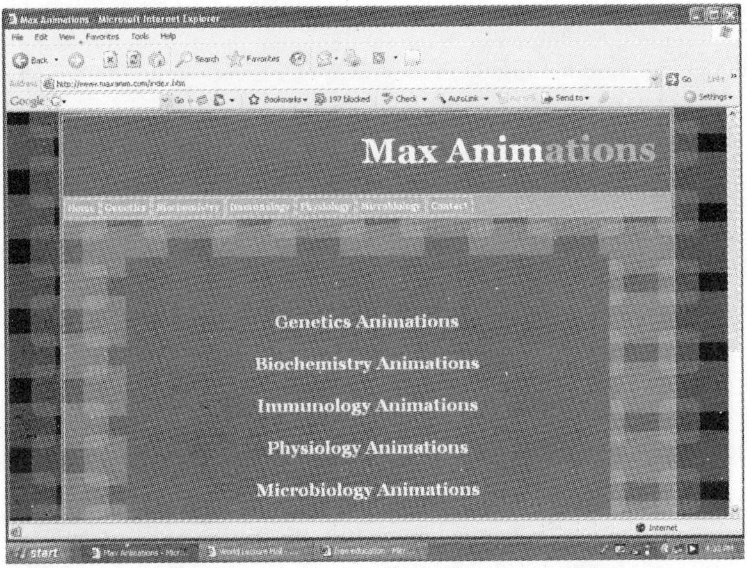

Knowledge @ Wharton (http://knowledge.wharton.upenn.edu)

This site offer free access to

1. Analysis of current business trends
2. Interviews with industry leaders and Wharton faculty
3. Article based on the most recent business research
4. Conference overviews, book reviews and link to relevant content
5. Searchable database of over 1500 article and research abstract etc.

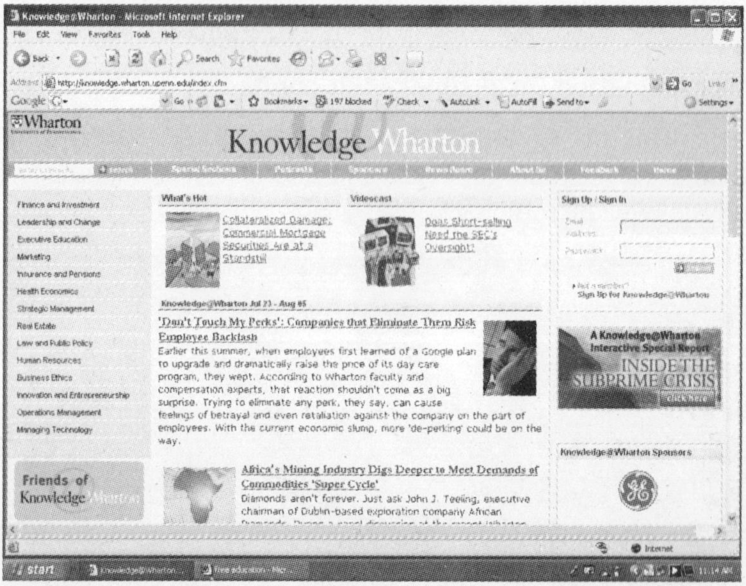

Harvard Business School Entrepreneurs (http://www.hbs.edu/entrepreneurs)

This is a video archives that captures insight from leading members of the schools entrepreneurial community. Moreover, there is also a forum named as HBS working knowledge for innovation in business practice, offering reader a first look at cutting-edge thinking and the opportunity to both influence and use these concepts before they enter main stream management practice

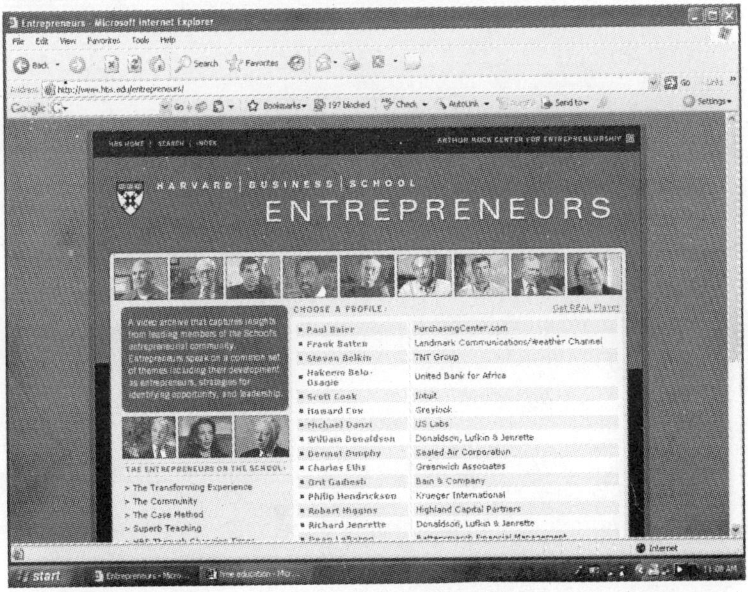

The creation of these e-contents, open courseware has mounted pressure and brings new challenges and opportunities for library and information professionals, as the eyes are now on them, to tap these courseware, analyze it as per their institute course content, and make it available for their clientele. It is the library and information professionals, who can direct, that what is available, where is available and how to make use of it, as they are assumed to have expertise in searching, organizing and disseminating information.

CONCLUSION

With the rapid pace of evolution in technology, competitive global economy, lack of skilled personnel and focus on knowledge management, e-learning is going to make a boom in India, this can also be judged by the clearance given by distance education council to IIMs and IITs to offer online courses. The debate on the success and survival of e-earning can continue till the cows comes home but one thing is sure that, e-learning can ensure consistency, reduce costs, and time and enable a richer learning experience.

REFERENCES

1. "A Lot of Hard Work." Times of India Delhi. Feb 04, 2008. http://epaper.timesofindia.com/APA26300/printArt.asp?SkinFolder=pastissues2. visited on : July 01,2008.
2. Allan, Barbara. *E-learning and Teaching in Library and Information Services.* Facet publishing, London. 200;247-253.
3. "At India Inc., IT is Learning Time." Times of India Delhi. June 14, 2007. http://epaper.timesofindia.com/APA26300/printArt.asp?SkinFolder=pastissues2. visited on : June 30.
4. "At Varsity, Books to be just a Click Away". Times of India Delhi., Mar 26, 2006.http://epaper.timesofindia.com/APA26300/printArt.asp?SkinFolder=pastissues2. visited on : July 01,2008
5. "Blended Learning Comes to DU." Times of India Delhi. Apr 07, 2008. http://epaper.timesofindia.com/APA26300/printArt.asp?SkinFolder=pastissues2. visited on : June 30, 2008.
6. "Bridging Distances." Times of India Delhi. June 04, 2007. http://epaper.timesofindia.com/APA26300/printArt.asp?SkinFolder=pastissues2. visited on : June 30, 2008.
7. "Click to Learn." Times of India Delhi. Dec 10, 2007. http://epaper.timesofindia.com/APA26300/printArt.asp?SkinFolder=pastissues2. visited on : June 30, 2008.
8. "Colleges Get Tech-savvy for GenX Students". Times of India

Delhi. July 04, 2007. http://epaper.timesofindia.com/APA26300/printArt.asp?SkinFolder=pastissues2. visited on : July 01,2008.

9. "Distance Learning is in." Times of India Delhi. Jun 06, 2005. http://epaper.timesofindia.com/APA26300/printArt.asp?SkinFolder=pastissues2. visited on : June 30, 2008.

10. "DU Goes Beyond Book, Blackboard." Times of India Delhi. Jan 10, 2008. http://epaper.timesofindia.com/APA26300/printArt.asp?SkinFolder=pastissues2. visited on : June 30,2008.

11. "DU Opens Eyes to Braille.." Times of India Delhi. Aug 19, 2006. http://epaper.timesofindia.com/APA26300/printArt.asp?SkinFolder=pastissues2. visited on : June 30,2008.

12. "Equipped to Learn." Times of India Ahmedabad. Sep 06, 2006. http://epaper.timesofindia.com/APA26300/printArt.asp?SkinFolder=pastissues2. visited on : June 30.

13. "IGNOU Goes Online." Times of India Delhi. Jun 16, 2008. http://epaper.timesofindia.com/APA26300/printArt.asp?SkinFolder=pastissues2. visited on : June 30.

14. Joshi, Sneha M., Pushpanadham, K and Khirwadkar, Anjali, 2002. "Knowledge Management through E-learning: An Emerging Trend in the Indian Higher Education System." *International Journal of E-learning:Corporate, Government, Healthcare, and Higher Education*. Vol. 1, no.3 : 47-54.

15. "Learning@Cyberspace". Times of India Nagpur. Apr 02, 2007. http://epaper.timesofindia.com/APA26300/printArt.asp? SkinFolder=pastissues2. visited on : June 30,2008.

16. "Learning through Fresh Delivery Modules". Times of India Delhi. July 02, 2007. http://epaper.timesofindia.com/APA26300/printArt.asp?SkinFolder=pastissues2. visited on : June 30.

17. "Legal Learning". Times of India Delhi. June 16, 2008 http://epaper.timesofindia.com/APA26300/printArt.asp?SkinFolder=pastissues2. visited on : June 30.

18. "Librarian : A Scholarly Profession.." Times of India Delhi. May 19, 2008. http://epaper.timesofindia.com/APA26300/printArt.asp?SkinFolder=pastissues2. visited on : July 01,2008.

19. "MIT Wants a Share of IITs' Courseware". Times of India Delhi. May 26, 2007. http://epaper.timesofindia.com/APA26300/printArt.asp?SkinFolder=pastissues2. visited on : July 01,2008.

20. "NCERT Introduces Multimedia CDs on Science". Times of India Delhi. Nov 11, 2004.http://epaper.timesofindia.com/APA26300/printArt.asp?SkinFolder=pastissues2. visited on : July 01, 2008.

21. "Robots Come to Classrooms." Times of India Delhi. Apr 28, 2008. http://epaper.timesofindia.com/APA26300/printArt.asp? SkinFolder=pastissues2.

22. Rosenberg, Marc J. 2001. *E-learning: Strategies for Delivering Knowledge in the Digital Age*. McGraw-hill, New York.

23. Sadik, Alaa, 2007. "The Readiness of Faculty Members to Develop and Implement E-learning: the case of an Egyptian University". *International Journal of E-learning: Corporate, Government, Healthcare, and Higher Education*. Vol. 6, no. 3, 433-454 p.

24. Shemla, Anat and Nachmias, Rafi, 2007. "Current State of Web-Supported Courses at Tel-Aviv University". *International Journal of E-learning: Corporate, Government, Healthcare, and Higher Education*. Vol. 6, no. 2, 235-246 p.

25. "Teaching through Technology." Times of India Delhi. Mar 31, 2008. http://epaper.timesofindia.com/APA26300/printArt.asp?SkinFolder=pastissues2. visited on : June 30, 2008.

26. Times of India Delhi. July 25, 2005 http://epaper.timesofindia.com/APA26300/printArt.asp?SkinFolder=pastissues2. visited on : June 30,2008.

27. "Virtual Blackboards". Times of India Delhi. Jan 24, 2007. http://epaper.timesofindia.com/APA26300/printArt.asp?SkinFolder=pastissues2. visited on : July 01,2008.

28. "Virtual Reality." Times of India Delhi. Sep 17, 2007. http://epaper.timesofindia.com/APA26300/printArt.asp?SkinFolder=pastissues2. visited on : July 01,2008.

29. Wang, Yu-mei, 2009. "Internet Uses in University Courses". *International Journal of E-learning : Corporate, Government, Healthcare, and Higher Education.* Vol. 6, no.2, 279-292 p.

30. "What does E-learning Mean." Times of India Pune. Mar 07, 2006. http://epaper.timesofindia.com/APA26300/printArt.asp? SkinFolder=pastissues2. visited on : June 30, 2008.

10

Challenges before the Library Profession in Acquiring and Managing Electronic Resources

Dr. Narender Kumar
Deputy Librarian,
Delhi University, Delhi

INTRODUCTION

The change in traditional document delivery services, from print to electronic, has come about very quickly, and libraries and information services have undergone significant transformation in order to effectively deliver electronic resources to the academic community. Moreover, the rapid advancement of information communication technology (ICT) has brought a revolutionary change in the information scenario giving rise to number of options to the users' community to handle varied information sources conveniently and effortlessly as a result of which e-resources have become the lively substance to the modern library's reserves in satisfying varied needs of students, teachers, and researchers with minimum risk and time.

Electronic resources are rapidly replacing print resources as the largest consumer of library and information center acquisition budgets. Logically, organizations want to evaluate the usage of electronic resources and incorporate the results into their decision making regarding resource acquisition, licensing and termination (as well as the related allocation of other library resources including staff and physical space). The current process for assessing the usage of electronic resources for a given institution, however, is extremely complicated, time-consuming, and highly unsatisfactory. Factors that contribute to the problem include:

- the diversity of resources and providers and the methods by which resources are provided to institutions and end-users;
- the diversity of mechanisms used to deliver usage statistics;
- the diversity of formats and methods of data transfer;
- the non-standardized, and often inefficient, presentation (structure, style) of usage data, which complicates integration with local data repositories and analysis systems; and;
- the fundamental incomparability of data across different providers and resources, which prevents useful local analysis (by cost centers or other functional groupings).

The development of online materials during the last decade compelled the discussion of why people would use an electronic version that appears to take longer to access than the print and may not be as easy to use. Therefore, it is the time for the information professionals to study the different key dimensions of electronic resources by identifying and addressing some of the issues relating to the use of e-resources.

FEATURES OF ELECTRONIC RESOURCES

No Physical Boundary

The user of a digital library need not to go to the library physically; people from all over the world can gain access to the same information, as long as an Internet connection is available.

Round the Clock Availability (24X7)

A major advantage of digital libraries is that people can gain access to the information at any time, night or day. The move to a networked environment has significantly increased the range of services and resources that the library provides its users. The library has become a twenty-four-hour-a-day access point to information services where users obtain services and resources on their terms and why they want such services.

Multiple Accesses

The same resources can be used simultaneously by a number of institutions and patrons. This may not be the case for copyrighted material: a library may have a license for lending out only one copy at a time; this is achieved with a system of digital rights management where a resource can become inaccessible after expiration of the lending period or after the lender chooses to make it inaccessible (equivalent to returning the resource).

Information Retrieval

The user is able to use any search term (word, phrase, title, name and subject) to search the entire collection. Digital libraries can provide very user-friendly interfaces, giving clickable access to its resources.

Preservation and Conservation

Digitization is not a long-term preservation solution for physical collections, but does succeed in providing access copies for materials that would otherwise fall to degradation from repeated use. Digitized collections and born-digital objects pose many preservation and conservation concern that analog materials do not.

Space

Whereas traditional libraries are limited by storage space, digital libraries have the potential to store much more information; simply because digital information requires very little physical space to contain them and media storage technologies are more affordable than ever before.

Added Value

Certain characteristics of objects, primarily the quality of images, may be improved. Digitization can enhance legibility and remove visible flaws such as stains and discoloration.

Up-To-Date Information

In the networked environment users get the updated information at any given time which is not possible in print environment.

Multimedia format

In the text format user can see or read one time of format at a time. In electronic format one can see text, watch the video on the given text, hear the same text in voice.

Interactive

With the advent of Web 2.0 technology the communication on WWW have became two ways. In the beginning the user can retrieve the information through net there were no provisions for interaction. However the Web 2.0 technology we can pose a question and will get the answer instantly. Even user can contribute in the development of the content of the web.

Special Services i.e. SDI, Alerts, etc

Each database has provision to provide alert services. The user can logon the respective database and enter his/her area of interest/research. Whenever there is new material on that particular area automatic alert will be provided by the vendor/publishers.

Easy Citations

All databases provide facilities of one or two citation manuals by which users can standardize the citation of the information if they want to cite the information in their research work.

Reduce the Cost of Paper and Ink

By using the electronic format lot of paper can be saved which could have been used in paper form to communicate the same information. In other words electronic resources are helping in to save the environment.

IMPACT OF ICT ON LIBRARIES

Technological revolution has changed the format of information resources and information seeking behavior of information users.

Collection to Connectivity

Earlier libraries emphasized for the development of collection in books and periodicals and made efforts to make all the documents physically available in the library needed by the users. However, these days' libraries make every efforts to satisfy the information need of its users by providing connectivity through computer without giving any importance to whether the documents are available in the library physically or not.

Ownership to Accessibility

Earlier libraries were paying to vendors/ publishers for getting the physical ownership of documents but these days libraries are paying bulk of its budget to have access to the information needed by its users. Libraries after paying amount do not get the ownership of documents but get only the access to the access for a period for which payment is made.

Aakar to Nirakar

In the traditional library, most library materials were housed in a physical library building, and users typically needed to come to the library to use its materials and services. Availability was an important concern because of the physical characteristics of the materials. In the networked library, however, library materials and services increasingly reside outside the physical library building. Earlier users scan the physical medium which they could see, touch and smell (Aakar) to have the required information whereas now a day they can have the required information without seeing, touching and smelling (Nirakar).

Real to Virtual

In traditional library environment there is need of space, building with four walls, furniture, space for reading room and many more physical items and users were required to visit the library personally to have the requisite material whereas in networked environment the library can provide required information without the forcing the users to visit the library personally. The libraries have been providing all information to the users without having the physical infrastructure as required in the traditional environment.

Paper to Pixel

Numbers of digitization projects have been undertaken throughout the world to convert the paper photograph, picture, text into pixel to be able to preserve them and provide access to the world.

More Physical Space to More Bandwidth

In order to satisfy the demand of Ranganathan's Fourth law of library science i.e. Save the Time of the Reader libraries demanded the centrally located place for libraries and functional building to save the time of the reader. However, in the networked environment libraries demand more bandwidth so that users' time can be saved by giving the access at faster speed.

Catalogue to Search Engine

The impact of ICT is so much on the functioning of the libraries that these days user wants that what ever documents (Print or Electronic) are available/accessible in the library should be searchable from a single platform/ window. Hence librarians have been searching for suitable search engines to meet the requirements.

INTERSTING FACTS ABOUT WEB

The nature of information delivery and consumption is changing. The ability to retrieve, organize, and store information with electronic sources will popularize the electronic resources. Even modern information technology provides easy and fast access for almost everyone to use the ever growing amount on Internet; there are some interesting facts about the www which are as follows:

- 4000 million unique websites
- Only 6% websites have Academic contents
- One web page has an average life of 75 days
- Google indexes less than 18% of total web pages
- Any body can upload web page but no authentication of information

(*Source:* Navbharat Times, 13/02/2010)

CHALLENGES

Planning

The best way for acquiring new electronic resources is to prepare a master list based on resources available in other institutes. Web sites of national and international institute can be

Ask the Faculty members for their requirements

In an academic library the faculty members may be requested to give their suggestion about the electronic resources to be acquired and which will help in teaching and research.

Before subscribing get a trial version of the resource

Ask the trial version of the electronic resources to be acquired for the library. After requesting for trial version inform the academic community about the trial period so that they can the resource.

Analyze trial usage and faculty recommendations

After the trail period is over ask the vendor to provide the usage statistics and analyse them and if found useful acquire it.

Pricing

Pricing is the most difficult part of electronic resources as there has been no fix price as in the case of print source. There are various modules like one time or per article base. Pricing on the bases of number of ID/password an institution needs. Pricing can be based on IP based in which the vendor considers FTP of the institute. While finalizing the prices the following measures can be taken by the librarian

- Form a negotiation committee which may include Librarian, Finance Officer, Academician, and Person from Computer Centre as members.
- If possible subscribe through consortia created by Government funded institutes like INDEST, UGCINFONET not through private consortia
- Always try to get the price they have offered to other institute
- If possible negotiate directly with publisher or aggregator not through agent.
- Decide the price cap (should not be more than 5% of negotiated price). It can be decided at the time of negotiation if institute plans to subscribed the resource more than one year.
- Negotiate Hard. Though you need the resource but don't show it. Tell them we can do without the resource.

Terms and Conditions

While negotiating for any electronic the terms and

conditions should be decided explicitly so that there would not be any problems. While deciding the terms and conditions the following may be consider:

Retention of Print Run: Whether the institution will be entitled to have print run of the source for archival purpose or not.

Consortia Subscription: What would be policy of the vendor in case the same electronic resource is made available to the institute through consortia. Whether the institute will have right to claim the payment of prorate basis or not.

Duplication with other Database: There are number of databases in which journals are common e.g. ABI/INFORM and Business Source Premier. What is the policy of the aggregator/vendors. Will they provide certificate that they have not charged price for the journal which is duplicate with the other database.

Perpetual Access : In case the institute stops the subscription the vendor/aggregator will provide the access for the period for the institute made the payment. This should be clearly mentioned in the terms and conditions.

Licensing

Licensing is another area on which librarian should be careful. The following points should be kept in mind while signing the license: The following points should be kept in mind:

- State clearly what access rights are being acquired
- Should recognize the intellectual property rights of both
- Should not hold the licensee (Library) for unauthorized uses of the licensed resource by its users

- Permanent use of a resource should allow the licensee (library) to copy data for the purpose of preservation and/or the creation of usable archival copy
- Should not require the licensee (library) to adhere to unspecified terms in a separate agreement between the licensor and a third party unless the terms are fully reiterated in the current license or fully disclosed and agreed to by the licensee (library).
- Governing Laws.
- Get the license vetted from the legal division.
- Only the administrative head or the person who has been authorized should sign the agreement.
- The Licensee shall not be responsible for the travel and related costs of the professionals for imparting training to the staff and users.
- UGC-INFONET and Delhi University outlines model draft (Annexure 1)

Low Usage

Despite the good spending on the electronic resources the users are not using extensively. There are number of reasons such as:

Lack of Awareness: Due to low computer literacy users are not aware about the availability of the electronic resources. This lack of awareness is more in social science and humanities than science stream.

Lack of Infrastructure: Another reason of low usage is lack of infrastructure like IIMs and IITs where the available of computer with internet connection is 1:1 whereas in other institutions this ratio is not there.

Effective Management of Resources: Libraries are not managing effectively the electronic resources they subscribe like preparation of A-Z list of periodicals available in electronic format.

Absence of federated search environment: Another reason of low usage is the non availability of the federated search environment as user has to open one database to another when he/she wants to search the different databases.

Promotion of Electronic Resources

The library should adopt the following measures to enhance the usage of electronic resources:

Information Literacy Programme: The library should conduct information literacy programme in which users should be made aware about the availability of electronic resources. They should also trained to maximize the use of electronic resources.

Enhance Computer Infrastructure: More and more workstations should be provided to the users for accessing the electronic resources with good bandwidth.

Attractive Home Page: The library should create a attractive home page for the electronic resources.

Federated Search Engine: The Library should provide federated search environment to the users so that they search the all databases through single window search.

Remote Login: If possible the institute should provide facilities for remote login so that users. There are number of open source software are available which facilitate remote login without breaching the contract e.g. Rewrite the URL Script.

Sustainability

Libraries in India have started spending huge amount on electronic resources. For example University of Delhi spent Rs. 34 per student on e-resources in 2004-05 which has gone up to Rs.2500/- per student in 2009-10. Despite the huge the spending libraries face problems in sustaining the existing database being subscribed the institute as an average increase in the resources is 20-25% per annum. For example subscription price of Chicago Manual of Style in 2006-07 was $450 and remain same in 2010 but in the library has pay 12% in terms of Rs as there is change in the exchange rate of the currency.

CONCLUSION

The evaluation of the usage of electronic resources can help determine the cost-benefit return of network electronic resources for collection development decisions; it can generate outputs for performance assessment; it can lead to the assessment of service quality; and it can contribute to outcomes assessment. For example, collecting, presenting and analyzing vendor-supplied, usage data for a library's networked electronic resources informs collection development decisions by generating cost/use data or market penetration metrics, that is, the percentage of the relevant population reached by the networked electronic resource.

ANNEXURE A : DRAF FOR AGREEMENT BETWEEN THE UNIVERSITY OF DELHI AND PUBLIHSER/SERVICE PROVIDER

1. Terms and Conditions of the Agreement

The licensors are expected to incorporate the following terms and conditions in their agreements. The University of Delhi and its faculties, departments, centers, schools and colleges is termed as "**Subscriber**", and the publisher/service provider is termed as "**Licensor**".

2. Access

2.1 The Licensor shall provide IP-enabled access to the subscriber to their e-resources. If there is any addition/deletion in the already provided IP Range the licensor will have to make necessary changes.

2.2. The licensor shall provide search, browse, view, and download facilities. The licensor will allow inter-library loan for print / softcopy of articles from their licensed e-resource on "not for profit" basis.

2.3. Licensor shall provide usage statistics reports on monthly basis to the University Librarian, DULS as per details provided under Para 9.0.

2.4. The user shall be bona-fied employee, faculty, student, researcher (full-time / part-time), alumni members and corporate members of the University of Delhi and that number shall be unlimited. Users shall be allowed unlimited access (preferably), view, search, browse, download and print the data for their use. Walk-in visitors who are physically present at the subscriber's site should also be allowed to use the resources.

2.5. The publisher would provide access to the new titles added during the contract period at no additional charge.

2.6. Subscribers may provide electronic links to the licensed materials from their web sites at journal level and licensor should provide help in doing so.

2.7. Subscriber should be allowed to download bibliographic records and abstracts in their local database (especially records for publications from their own faculty, staff and students) and full-text articles published by its faculty/students in its Institute's e-print archives.

3. Payment

3.1. Subscriber understands that different publishers / licensors / service providers have different pricing models. So, the fee for the access of e-journals shall be arrived differently depending on pricing model through mutually negotiable agreement.

3.2. The payment would be released only after certifying "access-enabled" certificate from different users. Multiple year agreements will be invoiced annually.

3.3. Whenever the agreement is entered into, the payment computation will be on "pro-rata basis" with effect from the date of contract entered into for remaining period of that calendar year. The subscription period may also be extended into non-calendar year, if mutually agreed.

3.4. If the payment is to be made in Indian currency to the representative of the publisher in India, the currency conversion shall be done on the TT bank selling rate as prevailing on the date of publisher's invoice.

4. Tenure

4.1. The agreement shall commence on the date of providing access and continue on annual basis or for a period as decided by the Subscriber.

4.2. Multiple-year agreements will automatically be renewed for successive one-year term unless either party gives notice of minimum one month to the other party in writing.

5. Back-issue rights

5.1. The licensor shall provide access to all e-resources with back volumes/date with a minimum period of five years base (calendar year) of full text of all the titles.

5.2. The new title or titles added during the contract period shall be provided at no additional charge along with their back issues.

5.3. Back-issues access would be provided for titles that are discontinued or merged with other titles during the contract period.

6. Archival Policy

6.1. The perpetual access to e-resources for the period of subscription along with their back-files offered during the subscription period would be preferred. In case, the resource is licensed on print based subscription, perpetual access should allow cross-sharing of subscribed resources amongst all subscribers.

6.2. On completion of every year, the publisher would provide the full-text of e-resources (e-journals/e-databases) for that year on prevalent formats, i.e. CD-ROM / DVD-ROM to the University of Delhi with the retrieval software for access on the network.

6.3. In case of termination of the agreement or on the expiry of the agreement, the Licensor shall provide the full text of the e-journals or e-databases for the period of agreement on the prevalent formats on CD-ROM, DVD, etc with the retrieval software for network access to University of Delhi.

6.4. In case of change in archival technology, the state-of-art archival technology shall be made available by the Licensor to subscribers at no extra cost for archival of full text data of e-journals to higher version of technology as and when it arrives.

7. Awareness Building and User Support

7.1 Licensor will inform University of Delhi about their user's meet/seminars to be organized in the country / in the region well in advance to enable the subscriber to participate free of cost in the event.

7.2 Licensor will provide adequate number of publisher's publicity material, brochure, posters and user support material in both print as well as on CD form, as applicable.

8. Training

8.1 The Licensor will conduct 'Train-the-Trainer' sessions for at least ten library and information science professionals to be named by the University of Delhi.

8.2 The Licensee shall, however, not be responsible for the travel and related costs of the professionals for attending such training programme.

8.3 The Licensor will provide the 'Train the Trainer' programme in the consolidated training programme along with the other publishers, if required. Subscriber will inform Licensor, the schedule of such training Programme.

8.4 The subscriber will not pay any charges to licensor for 'Train the Trainer' Programme towards travel/stay, etc.

8.5 Licensor will provide sufficient copies of the course manual in electronic and printed form at their own cost.

8.6 Licensor will inform the address and contact details of the 'Train the Trainer' to Subscriber for any help required by the users.

9. Usage Statistics

9.1 Licensor shall be required to submit the following 'COUNTER' complaint usage / statistics: shall be provided for

- Current month
- Previous month
- Cumulative for the current year
- Cumulative for the previous year(s)

9.2 Data as at (9.1) above shall be provided for each journal.

9.3 In case of any discontinuation or gap, the publisher shall inform the reason and the origin of discontinuation /gap.

9.4 The designated technical / administrative contacts from University of Delhi shall be given access to the publisher's server/database, where usage statistics is hosted. Licensor shall allow access to down load the statistics to designated contacts staff.

10. General Terms and Conditions (GTC)

10.1 In the event that access to E-journals/ database is stopped from the Licensor's end due to any problem, subscriber / member institution, etc. shall be allowed access for the same period / time as the breakdown, after the term of the contract or subscriber shall deduct the proportionate amount from the fees payable to the Licensor or the licensor shall refund the proportionate amount to the subscriber.

10.2 A notice of one month shall be provided by either side in the event of termination of contract.

10.3 If the licensor sells or otherwise transfers ownership of e-journals to another licensor it will provide non-exclusive copy along with of volumes in published and make it available through the licensor's site to subscriber. In case it does not happen, the amount shall be proportionately refunded to the subscriber.

10.4 University of Delhi recognizes the following obligations on its part:

10.4.1 Maintaining the integrity of the licensed products; and

10.4.2 Ensuring access to and use of licensed products is limited to authorized users;

10.5 The subscriber shall not be responsible for any sales tax, VAT or other taxes or any other license fee or any other hidden cost except the agreed invoiced amount.

10.6 The agreed terms and conditions can't be altered without mutual consent of both the parties.

10.7 Licensor will have to indemnify the subscriber for losses / claims / compensation caused/raised by third party with regard to the contract.

10.8 The licensor liability to subscriber shall be to a sum equal to the fee paid by subscriber if things go wrong on the part of Licensor.

10.9 The subscriber shall not be liable for breach of any of the terms of the agreement by any authorized user provided that subscriber did not intentionally assist in or encourage such breach or permit such breach to continue after having noticed thereof and provided reasonable cooperation to licensor(s) to prevent misuse.

10.10 Any kind of breach of agreement as a result of conditions beyond control such as a war, strike, fire, flood, governmental restrictions, power failures, damage, or destruction, act of God shall not be deemed as a breach of the contract agreement.

10.11 In case of closure or merger of any of the member institution, the print subscription of the particular member institution(s) will not be maintained.

10.12 In case of closure or merger of any of the member, the respective subscription/access costs will not be taken into account for payment or other fee chargeable by the licensor.

10.13 In case, access fee is based on the print subscriptions cost model, the year of signing the agreement will be base year for taking the print subscriptions cost into account to compute the access fee payable to licensor.

10.14 The publisher would not discontinue the access to e-resources on account of excessive downloads at subscriber's end. Instead, the publisher should devise mechanism to check excessive simultaneous downloads using robots or other mechanism. The publisher may also inform threshold for abuse of e-resource in terms of maximum number of downloads.

10.15 In the event that access to E-journals/ database is available through any consortia to the University of Delhi the licensor would refund the amount paid to them on prorate basis and University of Delhi will not be bound to purchase any other product in lieu of the amount to be refunded.

11. Governing Laws and Jurisdiction

11.1 The contract agreement shall be governed by the laws of India.

11.2 All disputes arising under the contract agreement shall be settled under the rules of the international arbitration court by one or more arbitrators in accordance with the said rules. The place of the arbitration shall be in New Delhi (India) and carried out in the English Language.

11

Latest Tools and Techniques for Automation, Networking and Creation of Digital Libraries and Role of National Informatics Centre

Pradip Kumar Upadhyay
Technical Director,
National Informatics Centre, New Delhi

ABSTRACT

To outline some of the latest developments in the field of library and information management. To make Library and Information science professionals aware about tools and technologies in the field.

INTRODUCTION

Libraries' traditional role has been providing books, learning and information and it is critical that we transpose that role into the digital world where a vast quantity of information is online and citizens, more than ever, need support in navigating through it. Changes in the market - such as the mass digitisation of content by Google and others, Web 2.0 technology and the advent of e-books - are changing how people want to receive and engage with information. Web sites have become the integral part of information sources. Dependency and visits to Library sites are also increasing day by day.

We have used the "Brick and Mortar" Libraries so far. With the emerging "Internet based Knolwedge Economy" through out the World, encompassing developed countries, developing conutries and least developed countries, impact of this "borderlessness" is felt. The global buildup of Internet connectivity and growing availability of inexpensive computing and communication devices have made the World Wide Web (WWW) a virtual continent that is borderless. This new freedom is attributed to the "Web 2.0 era" of services and applications that facilitate Internet Users easily share opinions and resources. Technologies are important tools, no doubt, but they are secondary to achieving the greater goal of promoting free and open access to knowledge (i.e., technologically open, socially open). Web 2.0 thus represents a paradigm shift in how people use the Web and its associated technologies for their advantages.

HOW DO LIBRARIES STILL MATTER IN INTERNET ERA?

Many predict that the digital age will wipe public bookshelves clean, and permanently end the centuries-old era of libraries. Despite their perceived obsoleteness in the digital age both libraries - and librarians - are irreplaceable for many reasons. Libraries are distinct from Internet, librarians are the most suited professionals to guide scholars and citizens toward a better understanding of how to find valuable information online. Indeed, a lot of information is online. But a lot is still on paper. Instead of regarding libraries as obsolete, government should increase funding for improved staffing and technology. Today, more than ever, libraries are extremely important for the preservation and improvement of our culture.

Not everything is available on the internet. Google is digitizing millions of books from the World's largest libraries. But even if Google does successfully digitize some of human knowledge, it is unlikely that some of contemporary authors and publishers will allow their works to be freely accessible over the internet. It is already prohibited by law to make copyrighted books fully accessible through Google Book Search; only snippets.

School Libraries and Librarians improve student test scores and perform better on reading and writing exams, this has been proved by studies and surveys. **Digitization is going to take a while, a long while.** How long will it take to index the world's knowledge? In 2002, it was boasted that Google could digitize approximately seven million books in six years. By 2007, they have managed to index a million books. At the rate of approximately half a million books per year, digitizing 100 million books would take about - 200 years.

Physical libraries adapt to cultural change. Eliminating libraries would cut short an important process of cultural evolution. Librarians are the irreplaceable counterparts to web moderators. The internet is a mess. A library provides a clear, standardized set of easily retrievable resources. Google gives 1 million hits in one second, but who wants these. Nobody practically browses results more than one or two pages. Libraries provide ten relevant requirements in 10 seconds unlike Google's 1 million in one second. Not everyone has access to the internet and can afford books. Instead of providing computer and connectivity to every individual of their own, libraries serve community in a better way if provided with shared many computers with Internet connectivity in their premises.

EMERGING TECHNOLOGIES

Because of googlization phenomenon of the content world, which started with dotcom boom, a perception has emerged that the electronic publishing and the web should will significantly reduce the cost of content. But the web based library sites giving information at User's desktop are more reliable as compared to Internet search engines. Internet search gives 10,000 or 10 lakh hits in one second, but users are not interested in browsing the huge set of result running over hundreds of pages making them confused. They want only relevant ten results which libraries in general provide at right time.

But of course, the technologies available help libraries serve better. To count few are the prevalent killer technologies being talked among library and information science field are

Digital Library/Electronic Library/Virtual Library

Open Source

Library on web

Library Automation

Electronic Scholarly Publication

Institutional digital Repository

Barcode

RFID

E-Books

E-Journals

Library Consortia

Database Management

Content Management

Web 2.0

XML

Blog/RSS/Poadcast/ Wikis

Some of the revolutionary changes in the field of library and information science are

Personal Computing Revolution

Electronic Revolution

Network Revolution

Cellular Revolution

Video Games Revolution

Security/Authentication Revolution

Hypertext Revolution

Customization Revolution

Government Information Revolution

EXAMPLES OF LIBRARY PRODUCTIVITY SOFTWARES

Tool	Examples
Library Management Software	Libsys, Liberty, KOHA, eGranthalaya, SOUL, NewGenLib, Evergreen, etc
Digital Library Software	ContentDM, LSPremia, DSpace, Greenstone, Fedora, Sharepoint, etc
Word Processor	MS Word, Corel Word Perfect, Open Office write
Spreadsheet	MS Excel, Open office Cale, Google Spreadsheet, Simple Spreadsheet
Database management	MS Access, MS SQL Server, IBM DB2, Oracle, PostgreSQL, MySQL
Presentation Software	Open office Impress, MS Powerpoint, Apple Keynote, Harvard Graphics
Email	MS Outlook and Oulook Express, Mozilla Thunderbird, Opera M2 (gmail is not a software at your computer)
Web Browser	MS Internet Explorer, Mozilla Firefox, Google Chrome, Opera Presto
Chat	Microsoft Live Messanger, Yahoo Messanger, Google GTalk, Trillian, Pidgin
Developers Software	MS ASP.Net, VB.NET, PHP, Java, Perl,
Web Publishing	MS Frontpage, Dreamweaver, NVU, Javascript
Scanning/Reprographic	FineReader, Omnipage, Scansoft PDF Converter, Readiris

FIVE GENERATIONS OF COMPUTING

Gene-rations	Timeline	Major Event	Characteristics
1	1946-1958	Vacuum Tubes	Mainframe era begins
2	1958-1964	Transistors	Mainframe era expands and UNIVAC is updated with transistors

3	1964-1990s	Integrated circuits	Mainframe era ends and personal computers era begins
4	1990s-2000	Multimedia and low cost PCS	Personal Computers era endsLow cost, high performance integrated video, audio and data
5	2000-present	Widespread internet accessibility	Interpersonal computing era endsInter networking era begins Broad variety of devices

E-BOOKS, E-JOURNALS, E-LENDING AND E-PROCUREMENT

There are new and exciting opportunities around digital lending. With the launch of a number of different e-reading devices, digital reading is growing in the public consciousness where downloadable audio books are already fully established. E-books will enable library services to remain relevant in a market where people are using mobile devices to access information and entertainment and will provide a new opportunity to reach people who may not visit their local library building regularly, but who would like to borrow e-books from home.

There are different models for purchasing eBooks, eJournals or databases.

- Publishers are directly selling their eBooks to libraries and readers. For example, Wiley, Elsevier, Springer, Sage, etc.
- But like vendors supplying books and journals, aggregators and vendors are also purchasing contents from many publishers and sell these products of eBooks and journals to libraries. Examples are , NetLibrary, MyiLibrary, EBSCO, Safari Books Online, Books24x7, and many more.
- Majority publishers provide their online versions free along with print subscription/purchase

- Contracts for use of content are negotiated on an individual library basis with either publishers directly or third-party suppliers who negotiate terms of use with publishers and bundle deals for library services. eBooks may be subscribed for one year or purchased for perpetual.
- Access to these eBooks and eJournals is available majority on institutional public IP ranges. But some are also providing on userid and passwords.

RADIO FREQUENCY IDENTIFICATION (RFID)

One of the areas where RFID has been a cost effective deployment is within library systems, where, due to the high value of individual books and journals and the many ways in which each tag can deliver value (e.g. issue/returns, stocktaking etc.), the one-off cost of a tag is easily off-set by overall cost savings and efficiency gains. It is more useful and advanced than barcode technology. RFID is in demand where heavy transactions are there and objects are moving. For example, RFID tag can be put on a moving car and this car can be identified using RFID reader attached to gate or antennae.

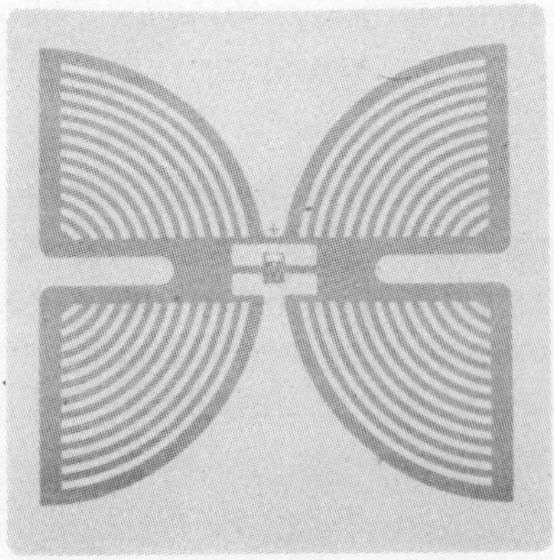

RFID Tag

The radio frequency part of RFID is the communication medium between tags and readers. With passive RFID tags, radio frequency is also used to deliver power to the tag, as they do not have on-board power systems.

Gate Antennae

Key Features of RFID at Libraries

- Member Records Management
- Library User ID Authentication
- Generate loan history for particular member
- Computerized Isuue/Return
- Allows to Issue or Return several books simultaneously
- Strict Inventory tracking & management
- Identify and sort books in accordance to their branch and category numbers as well as shelf locations

- **Theft Detection**
- Capability/Anti-theft Management
- Multi-item detection
- Library staff is alerted immediately when unborrowed books passes through the theft detection gates through an alarm system
- Would-be thieves are detected by physical presence at gate.

Myths of Digital Library, e-Library and Virtual Library

A **digital library** is a library in which collections are stored in digital formats (as opposed to print, microform, or other media) and accessible by computers. The digital content may be stored locally, or accessed remotely via computer networks. A digital library is a type of information retrieval system.

Meaning of a Digital Library is different for different people, organizations and communities. For a school student a Digital Library is collection of digital documents, database, video games and leaning materials accessible via computer network. For a space scientist collection may be available over Internet in the form of GIS and CAD data, satellite imagery, video gallery and so on so forth. For a farmer Digital library is a collection of information over a portal in the form of Government information, Land records, agriculture market information, etc. In a nutshell, Digital Library is a collection of information which is digitized, organized for a group of people or community, gives users power they had never with traditional libraries.

- Many consider Internet as digital library. Internet contains many more features and services including digital library.
- Is Digital libraries cheaper than print libraries? Overall development of library information system is long term agenda and cost intensive.
- Automated library is digital library. But it is more than automation.
- We can't scan and digitize the copyrighted print documents available in libraries without the prior permission and build digital library. Many legal issues are associated with the development and use of digital

libraries. Intellectual property rights are a major concern, others are authenticity of information resources, and privacy and security of users and institutions. Librarians, Publishers, lawyers and Governments over the years formulated regulations that control the intellectual property rights of owners of materials. Digitizing our own publications and contents and creating digital libraries is well within copyright. Sometimes many people download the licensed contents from Digital libraries and transmit them over Intranet and Internet without permission that causes legal problems.

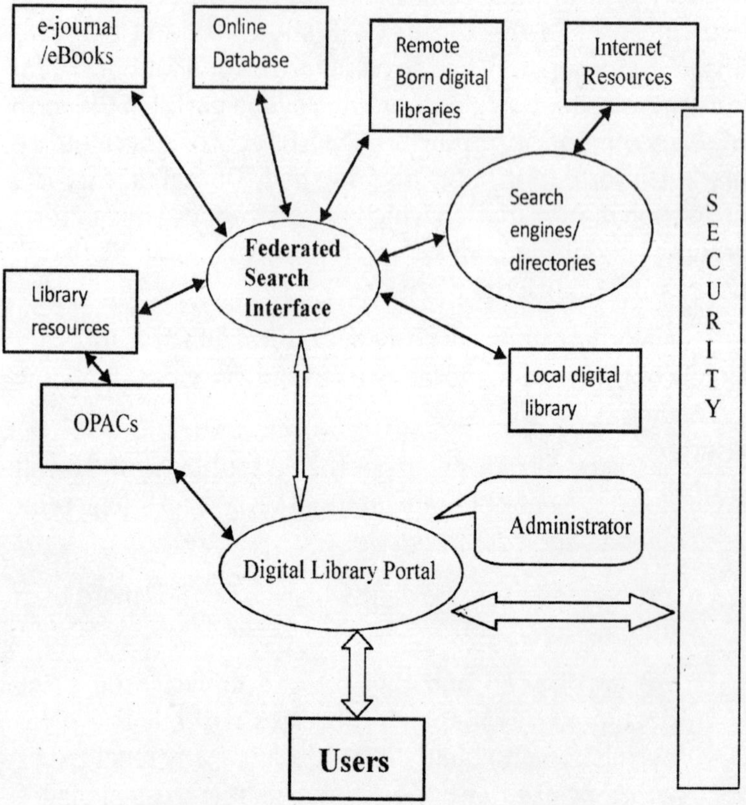

Figure: Conceptual design of a digital library

ROLE OF NATIONAL INFORMATICS CENTRE (NIC) FOR MODERNIZATION OF LIBRARIES IN INDIA

National Informatics Center (http://home.nic.in) of Government of India has been playing a pioneering role in propagating 'IT-led Development' facilitating rapid economic growth and socio transformation in India, by setting up a countrywide satellite based VSAT network (NICNET), first of its kind among the developing countries, linking 600 District Administration, 28 State Secretariats, and seven NCT/UT Administration. At present NIC is the only Government organization in India offering network services over KU-band (TDMA, FTDMA, DAMA and SCPC) VSATs, Wireless Metropolitan Area Networks (MAN) and Local Area Networks(LANs) with NICNET gateway for Internet resources, State of Art Video Conferencing facilities, e-Governance and e-Commerce, Multimedia Information system, Geographical Information System (GIS). NIC has functioned as Network Infrastructure Facility Provider (NIFP), Network Service Provider (NSP), Application Service Provider, and Content ASP.

e-Granthalaya (http://egranthalaya.nic.in) is an agenda of National Informatics Center for library automation and networking and support the vision of India a Knowledge based society. NIC has come up with a product also, named 'e-Granthalaya. The objectives of eGranthalaya agenda is

- Networking of 5 lakh Libraries and converting them into "digital Libraries" will be the step towards India becoming a Knowledge Society
- National Union Catalog of both digital and non-digital content
- Content Delivery to Grass root level
- Digital Library

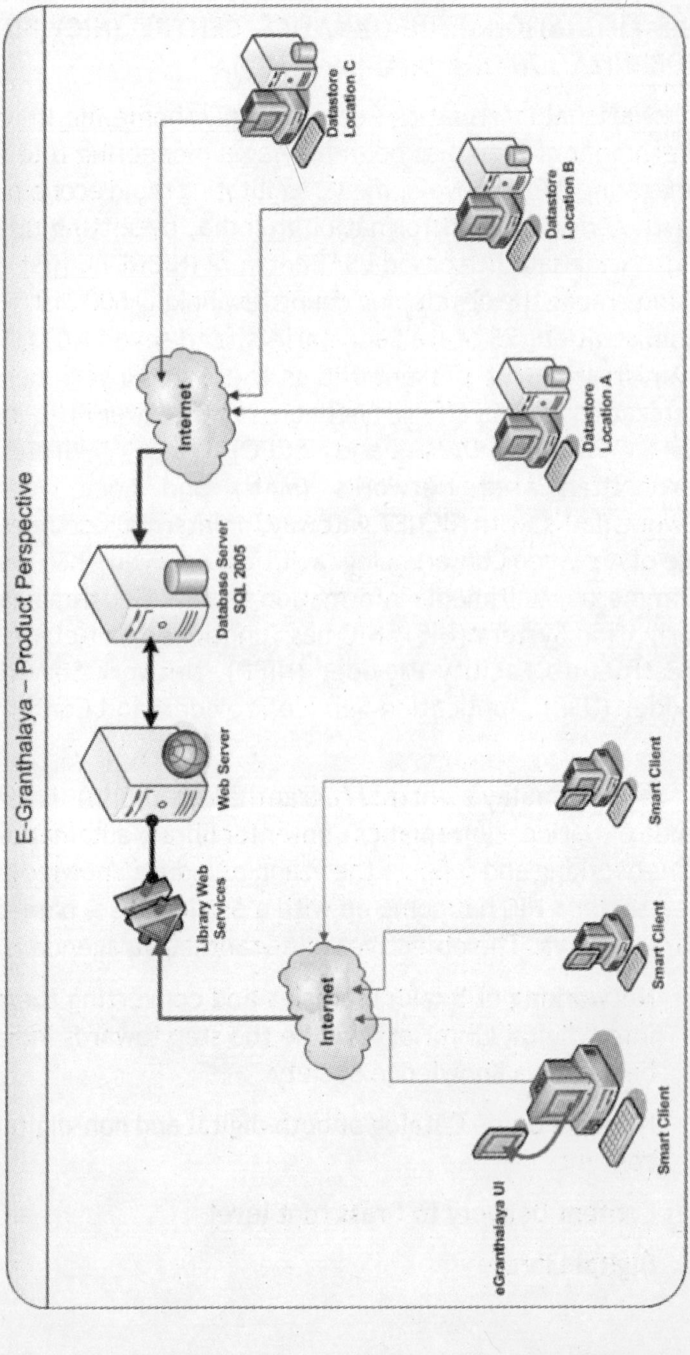
E-Granthalaya – Product Perspective
Library Web Services
Web Server
Database Server SQL 2005
Internet
Datastore Location A
Datastore Location B
Datastore Location C
Internet
eGranthalaya UI
Smart Client
Smart Client
Smart Client

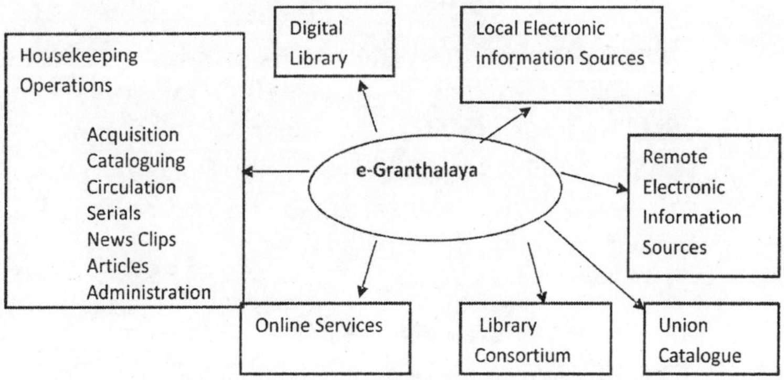

e-Granthalaya is distributed FREE to all the Government Libraries with free support for installation, training, up-gradation, etc. Training is organized regularly various NIC Centres and user premises.

BASIC REQUIREMENTS IN IMPLEMENTING LIBRARY TECHNOLOGIES TODAY

- Introducing IT, in any way, usually gives opportunities (and problems) beyond the initial application.
- Always remember that people are the most important part of any system, automated or otherwise. Decide the implementation strategy either by hiring ad-hoc manpower or hire outsourced agency. Support is very important either in a free or Open source or commercial applications.
- There should be a review mechanism for hardware and softwares at regular interval say three- four years .
- Decide mode of implementation. For example, software applications may be implemented in a single machine, in Client server mode, or network mode. But ideally, applications today must be deployed in

network mode so that it may be accessed from anywhere on Internet/ Intranet

- Choose software first, then hardware. Procure Server side OS (Linux or Windows 2008 for server and windows7 for clients), Database software(MS SQL server, or PostgreSQL, MySQL, or Oracle), Library software, Office Suite(Like MS office), Utility softwares (Like Anti virus, etc)
- Procure Hardware such as Server, clients machines, printers, UPS, Scanner and LAN equipments, Barcode printers and Scanners
- Libraries must be part of an institutional LAN . Do it in consultation with your network and computer centre.
- Essential that the catalogue database is accessible on your Library web site from workstations anywhere in the institution . That means you require Database and web hosting on Internet Service Provider like NIC, ERNET, CDAC, or private providers based in India or abroad. Normally these days it is to host the library's database on a public domain web server so that users can search the database even from their homes or hostel rooms or on the move.
- Build your library web site. But now prefer library portal instead of static web site. Portal is gateway that provides a single point of entry to information and tools. Link all the related applications and activities of library and organization with this portal. Example, make a portal using software - Drupal, Link this with library software eGranthalaya and Digital repository software DSpace. Below is picture for this:

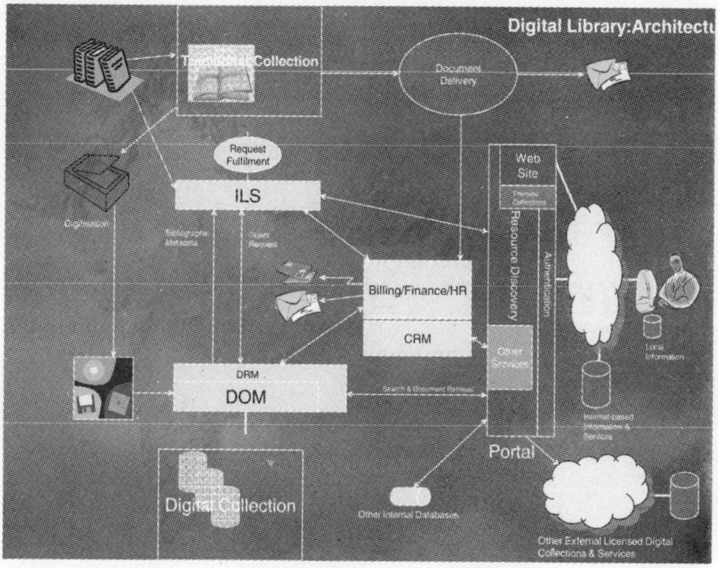
Digital Library:Architectu
Collection
Document Delivery
Request Fulfilment
ILS
Web Site
Resource Discovery
Authentication
Billing/Finance/HR
CRM
DRM
DOM
Other Services
Portal
Digital Collection
Other Internal Databases
Other External Licensed Digital Collections & Services

12

Management of Library & Information Services

Monika Aggarwal
Assistant Professor, Shah Satnam ji P.G.Girls'College, Sirsa Haryana 125055

ABSTRACT

Management of library and information services is a growing development in our country. How do the libraries at large institutions management of library & information services to a diverse community of users in an increasingly digital and complex environment? This paper suggests that with management capabilities of librarians can be very effective in applying their skills to the managing process in libraries. This will give a good image to library and users satisfaction also. This paper discusses and emphasizes the need for the adoption of management approach by the libraries to augment their financial resources and exploit new information technology to provide better information support to the users. This Also discusses on the problems in implementing management concept to library and information services.

INTRODUCTION

As information technologies, information systems and information networks have been developing, Digital libraries are increasingly promoting in the third millennium. As a result of such a development in the information services, libraries can be considered as a part of world or national network, playing a determinant role in the formation of scholarly relationships among researchers and societies. Consequently, moving from printed to digital environment is so deep and extensive that it mainly has been leading to changing nature of libraries as well as library science. In fact, libraries and information professionals have been faced a new paradigm; so, planning and anticipating library affairs have been challenged. Because of this, libraries especially their managers are thinking about restructuring and reengineering traditional services. In addition, the managers are concerned for how phenomenon Digital Libraries can be effectively managed so that not only they can meet the main mission of libraries to the society and human's cultural heritage, but also using innovations could provide information life cycle from creation to dissemination with more speed, scope, currency, efficiency, effectiveness, quality and productivity. For a library service to be successful there must be buy-in from the clients that the tools or databases are worthwhile. They must understand what the services are, and be enthusiastic about how they will be helpful. Hiring computer literate people helps libraries develop innovative management techniques.

Library and Information Science schools should emphasize courses that teach technical skills, including computer programming, in the context of building collections, disseminating information, and spreading the word about new databases or increased functionality. As we have seen, the web offers a unique environment whereby information services can be brought to life, and new methods for disseminating customized reports can be explored. It is particularly important for large organizations to make use of the web. Without library staff equipped to master the software and programming required to create these tools, the library misses opportunities to both publicize and customize information for users.

Management of library & Information services is the process of forecasting, planning, organizing, directing and controlling of library services that create the satisfaction of library and the customer.

The *DELOS Digital Library Reference Model* defines a digital library as:

An organization, which might be virtual, that comprehensively collects, manages and preserves for the long term rich digital content, and offers to its user communities specialized functionality on that content, of measurable quality and according to codified policies.

Management of library & Information services requires careful planning and begins with understanding the mission of library. It can help in developing the mission of the library, establishing a positive image for the library in the community, and determining the best way to provide services to users.

MAIN CONTENTS OF DIGITAL LIBRARY

1. Staff: one of the vital elements of success dynamism is specialized human resources via librarians. It should be noted that specialized staff is not simply limited to the librarians including catalogers, indexers and archivists but because of nature of Digital Libraries, other fields of particularly computer science are also involved. As a result of emergence of digital environment and navigation of Digital Libraries, librarians' traditional skills have changed and so librarians are faced by new functions. Hence, from managerial perspective, survival secret is to be flexible and to develop librarians' skills.

Skill and educations needed for Digital Libraries Staff

Web technology : library staff should be known to web technology otherwise they can't find any information.

Familiarity with web search tools : If library staff is familiar with web search tool than only they guide user.

Formulation of search strategies: They should be able to make strategies that how user can easily search what they want to search.

Evaluation of websites: By evaluation of websites they can easily know that now a days what pattern is going on so that users may feel satisfy.

Guidance and education of users: New users don't about the new technology of library. So it is the responsibility of library staff to guide them.

Analysis and interpretation of information: sometimes users don't have time so library staff has to give analytical information to user.

Integration of network resources: Network resources should be integrated so that users can use more resources.

Cataloguing and organizing digital information: Digital information should be in organized way. By this users get information in very less time.

Indexing & Abstracting: user can easily find that information what he need.

Information literacy (plus literacy of computer and network): Without literacy of computer & network digitization of library is impossible.

Admittedly, above suggested skills are not exhaustive; so, for further reading as well as more familiarity with necessary competencies for digital librarians, it is recommended to consult tasks, the requisite knowledge and skills suggested by Urs (2002)

CHARACTERISTICS FOR DIGITAL LIBRARIES' LIBRARIAN

For success of digital library Librarian should have some characteristics:

1. Multifaceted Knowledge

It means that the knowledge of the digital librarians should not be confined to a single field. Instead it should cover varied subjects such as library science, computer science, some specific technologies, and communication science and so on.

2. Intense Information Awareness.

- Have the consciousness to add value to the information;
- have the consciousness to offer information service actively;
- be good at finding useful information;
- be quick to respond to outside sources;

3. Tremendous Personality

- Good imagination and foresight: Future is uncertain but by good imagination & foresight good strategies can be made.
- Innovation intention: It will help to search & adopt new things.
- High team spirit: By this library environment will be peaceful.

- High flexibility: A librarian's nature should be flexible so that he adopts changes easily.
- Propensity to take risks: According to management more risk, more profit.
- Good interpersonal and negotiating skills: By this skill librarian can communicate very well with other people.
- Changeability (change management): Management technology can be changed according to situation so this feature is also must.
- Capacity to learn constantly: Knowledge will be update.
- Coping skills especially problem-solving one: for survive in competitive environment librarian must be coping skills.
- Crisis management: for surviving in dynamic, changing & competitive environment crisis management knowledge is must.
- Respect to professional ethics: It is moral responsibility of librarian that he must be respect to professional ethics.

Finance: Finance plays a very important role in the success of Library. But finance is a limited resource. By management only we can optimum utilization of finance.

Library Material: Now library material is not only available in the printed form such as books, but also in form of Cds, Videos, auto digital products or we can say in electronic form.

Users: Without users there is no use of Library. In Modern World users are not limited up to a particular area while they can be from anywhere in the world. So large number of users means more responsibility of librarian.

NEED FOR MANAGEMENT OF LIBRARY & INFORMATION SERVICES

Scarcity of resources: Some Library resources are limited for example Finance on the other hand finance is very important for library. By the help of management we can optimum use of finance.

Easily and rapidly avail facilities: By good management users get facility very easily.

Customer's requirements: Customer's requirement can be fulfill in very less time.

Beneficial to library image: If Digital library managed in good manner so it will be beneficial to library image.

BARRIERS TO MANAGEMENT OF LIBRARY & INFORMATION SERVICES

Limited Resource of Funds: Finance is a limited resource but it is very important for digital library. Due to finance problem some library can not fully digital.

Illiteracy of library staff: All library staff is not familiar with computer. They don't know how information can be received from computer.

Lack of Training: Digital library is not very old concept so everywhere its training is not possible. Often librarians do not promote library services due to lack of training and management knowledge.

Meaningless doubts: Generally users think that it's very difficult to get information while its not.

CONCLUSION

Digital libraries are treated as determinant information centers, libraries especially their managers are thinking about how Digital Libraries can be effectively managed. So, the present article aims to provide managers of Digital Libraries with an approach. Accordingly, some skills, instructional programs and qualities needed both for users and staff of Digital Libraries with which they can interact more effectively with new technologies. In fact, this paper emphasizes on educational function of DLs and thus offers an approach for its implementation from managerial standpoint.

REFERENCES

Bawden, D., 2005. Education and training for digital librarians: a Slovenia/UK comparison. *Aslib Proceedings: new information perspectives*, vol.57, no.1, pp85-98

Candela, L., The DELOS Digital Library Reference Model - Foundations for Digital Libraries. Version 0.98 Accessed February 2008.

Chang, N. and Hopkinson, A. 2006. Reskilling staff for digital libraries. ICADL (International Conference on Asian Digital Libraries), pp. 531-532.

Choi, Y. and Rasmussen, E., 2006. What is needed to educate future digital librarians? *D-Lib Magazine*. vol12, no.9

Greenstein, Daniel I. and Thobrin, Suzanne Elizabeth, 2002. *The Digital Library: a Biography. Digital Library Federation Access on* June 25, 2007

Isfandyari Moghaddam, A.R., 2009. Managing digital Llibraries in the light of staff and users: an approach. January / June, 2009 *International Journal of Information Science and Management*, vol. 7, no. 1, pp 31-40

Joint, N., 2003. Staff development and training in the digital library environment. *Library Review*. vol. 52, no. 9, pp. 417-421

Macleod, R.A. and Chiware, E.R.T., 1993. Lessons to be learned: Information Technology training in a developing country academic library. *Library Management*. vol. 14, no. 6, pp. 24- 30

Missingham, R., 2006. Library and information science: Skills for twenty-first century professionals. *Library Management*. vol 27, no.4-5, pp. 257-268.

Mullins, J. 2001. People-centered management in a library context. *Library Review*. Vol. 50, no. 6, pp. 305-309

13

Digital Library & Related Research Issues

V N Shukla
Gour Mohan
Natural Language Processing Lab, Centre for Development of Advanced Computing (Ministry of Communications & Information Technology)

ABSTRACT

With the rapid growth and spread of the reach of the internet the shape of the content and information is changing from printed to electronic. Millions of books and rare manuscripts have been stored in digital media. Till now the focus of the digital library initiative has been to make the content available digital form. This paradigm shift needs to be supported by number of technologies to make the benefits available to the masses. This paper highlights some of research issues which need to be addressed in the future to keep the momentum alive.

Keywords : Digital Library of India, Digital Library, Web Interface, Accessible Digital Library

INTRODUCTION

India is a truly multilingual country with 22 constitutionally recognized languages, 10 scripts and 1652 languages in total comprising of 350 major languages. People residing in different parts of country share languages and culture. This linguistic diversity supports the fact that India has a rich cultural heritage. In the last decade, India has witnessed tremendous socio-economic and institutional change in all sectors due to advancement in Information Technology. In the digital world, libraries have emerged as means of creation and dissemination of knowledge.

CDAC, Noida has been carrying out the digital library work under the projects such as Digital library Mega Center, Digitization of old and rare manuscripts, books and magazines at Varanasi and other projects at Uttranchal, President's House and digitizing the material pertaining to Mahatma Gandhi.

Under the Digital libraries projects task has been being carried out at various libraries across the country namely Gurukul Kangri Vishvidyalaya, Hardwar, Lal Bahadur Shastri National Academy of Administration, Delhi University, Indian Agricultural Research Institute (IARI), Birla Institute of Technology and Science Pilani, Jamia Millia University, National Council of Educational Research and Training (NCERT) and work has already been completed at the following centers Dayal Singh Library, Association of Indian Universities, Indian Council for Cultural Relations (ICCR), Association of Indian Universities, The Energy and Resources Institute (TERI).

These centers/libraries are located in different regions of Northern India, and have different types of content with them like Gurukul Kangari and BITS Pilani have rare content in Hindi, Sanskrit while ICCR and Jamia Millia University has manuscripts in Arabic, Persian, Urdu, Pashto etc.

DIGITAL LIBRARY

Digital Library may be defined as "organized collections of digital information. They combine the structuring and gathering of information, which libraries and archives have always done, with the digital representation that computers have made possible." - Lesk, 1997. Few others define it as "Digital libraries are organizations that provide the resources, including the specialized staff, to select, structure, offer intellectual access to, interpret, distribute, preserve the integrity of, and ensure the persistence over time of collections of digital works so that they are readily and economically available for use by a defined community or set of communities." - Digital Libraries Federation (DLF) [1]

Digital Library (DL) vs Traditional Library

- DL provides efficient & qualitative services by collecting, organizing, storing, disseminating, retrieving and preserving the information.
- DL supports preservation besides making information retrieval & delivery more comfortable.
- DL provides online access to historical and cultural documents whose existence is endangered due to physical decay.
- Digital libraries necessarily include a strong focus on the management of digital content.

Traditional libraries have been focusing for long on the preservation and management of content in physical forms.

Digital Library work Progress : CDAC Noida

As mentioned above the digital library work has been carried out by CDAC, Noida at different libraries/centers and about 21 million pages have been scanned so far. To make the content accessible to masses through Internet, a portal been developed and being continuously updated for use by different segment of users.

Digital Library: Research areas

Full Text search

Web interface is a computer software system for organizing and facilitating collaborative creation of documents and other content. The information in the form of manuscripts/ books/ magazines available was confined to the library where it was physically kept. The paper quality was deteriorating and it was difficult to read the information. The following process is followed before putting the documents on the web for masses.

The manuscripts/ books/ magazines are scanned, cleaned for noise and supported with metadata information before putting in database so that the information stored is readable and searchable. Once the manuscripts are available in the digitized form, multiple users can access it from the web interface at the same time and any information can be reproduced in the form of print. The information can be reproduced and used by people without having to refer the original manuscript. Through use of interface, images can be zoomed to any scale as per user requirement for easy access to information. The information in digitized form can be downloaded and referenced later or printed in the book form for future reference.

The features of the web interface are one can search the book/manuscript by creator/author, Title or by the date of publication. The full text search is only available on the English texts which are OCRed. In text retrieval, full text search refers to a technique for searching a computer-stored document or database; in a full text search, the search engine examines all of the words in every stored document

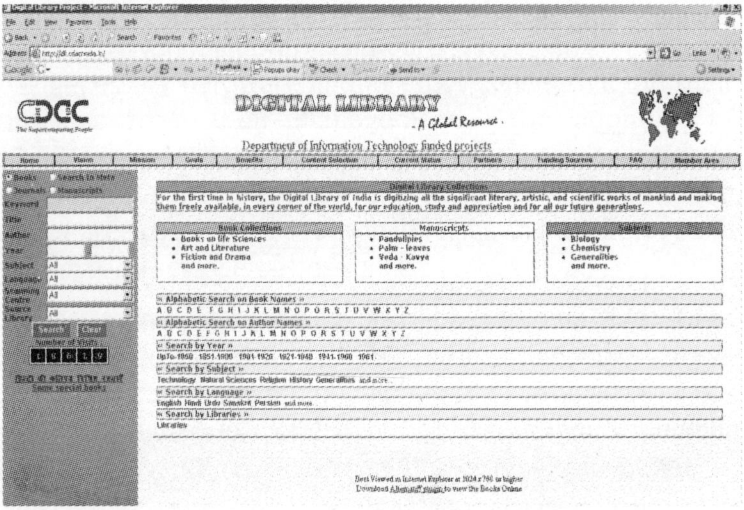

Fig. 1. "Digital Library of India (www.dli.cdacnoida.in)"

as it tries to match search words supplied by the user. Full-text searching techniques became common in online bibliographic databases.

The most common approach to full text search is to generate a complete index or concordance for all of the searchable documents. For each word (eliminating stop words or non-functional words) an entry is made which lists the exact position of every occurrence of it within the database of documents. From such a list it is relatively simple to retrieve all the documents that match a query, without having to scan each document. For Indian languages OCR and full text indexing is not supported by popular databases but the work is in progress in this direction also.

Spell checking and 'Did you mean'

The user interface needs to be improved and new features needs to be incorporated like spell check facility and highlighting of query words in the search results. The user click data can be a good source for better analysis of feedback and query log needs to be analyzed. The queries needs to be passed through the spell check module and if some error is detected the user may be shown the alternatives to select from.

Transliteration and Romanization schemes

Census 2001 reveals that a large chunk of population know more than one language. This has created a need for transliteration tools which can convert text written in one language script to another Indian language script. Many such conversions may need mapping of language script data to human and machine understandable intermediate form.

With Google and other transliteration tool people feel at ease of writing digitally in Indian languages using English script. However, among many ways of transcribing there is no consistency.

The above requirements create the need of having one standardized way of Roman Transcription scheme for Indian Scripts. This relates to the written languages, not to the spoken languages. Although this will often approximate the pronunciation of a language, that remains a secondary consideration.

Cross Lingual Search

Indian languages have comparatively lesser amount of data available over the net. Cross Lingual Information Retrieval systems come to the rescue of such situations where desired result is not fetched in the language of search input. CLIR systems take the advantage of the multi-lingual knowledge of users and present the results in second or third language of which the user is aware of, which is a better option than a null or not desired result. Such situations become more prevalent when search is focused towards queries related to regional information e.g. tourism specific queries related to smaller towns of a province.

Accessibility and speech interfaces

People with disabilities are often restricted in accessing the World Wide Web content. This is because of the poor web design. Access to web content is sometimes more critical for people with disabilities who can make use of particular digital formats only because they are print-disabled.

The Digital Library portal needs to be made compatible to the W3C's Web Content Accessibility Guidelines. The website if compatible can be used by people with disabilities such as:-

- Vision, hearing, movement, or may not be able to process some types of information easily or at all.
- Difficulty in reading or comprehending text.
- not able to use a keyboard or mouse.
- A text-only screen, a small screen, or a slow Internet connection.
- They may not speak or understand fluently the language in which the document is written.
- May be in a situation where their eyes, ears, or hands are busy or interfered with (e.g., driving to work, working in a loud environment, etc.).
- They may have an early version of a browser, a different browser entirely, a voice browser, or a different operating system.

Future research areas include making the content more accessible by introducing indexing, screen reading facility and making the website compatible to WCAG guidelines, and provide access to the website through mobile phones as an extension of the existing web.

A screen reader is a software application that attempts to identify and interpret what is being displayed on the screen. This is then presented to a blind user as speech (by text-to-speech) or by driving a braille display. Screen readers are used by people with little or no functional vision: people with some vision often use screen magnifiers. Many English screen reader programs are available in the market. For Indian languages these have yet to see the light of the day.

ACKNOWLEDGMENTS

Most of the projects discussed in the paper has been funded by Department of Information Technology, Ministry of Communications and Information Technology, Govt. of India and supported by IISc Bangalore. We would like to thank Prof. Raj Reddy, CMU, USA, Prof. N. Balakrishnan, IISc Bangalore & Dr. George Varkey, Executive Director, C-DAC, Noida for constant support, guidance and conducive environment for this work.

REFERENCES

1. www.ffzg.hr/infoz/lida/lida2000/dlib_evaluation.ppt
2. Shukla, V.N., Arora, Karunesh Kr. and Gugnani, Vijay, 2004. *Digital Handling of National Library,* ICOLNIS.
3. Digital Library activities in India. Available at http://www.dli.ernet.in
4. http://www.dlib.org/dlib/october02/fox/10fox.htm
5. Golub, Koraljka. Digital Library and the Blind and Visually Impaired.
6. http://www.w3.org/TR/WAI-WEBCONTENT/
7. Shukla, V.N. and others, 2005. *Digital Library Research : A developer's Perspective*. China, Zhejiang University.
8. Cleveland, Gary. Digital Libraries: Definitions, Issues and Challenges. Available at http://www.ifla.org/VI/5/op/udtop8 /udtop8.htm
9. Shukla, V.N. Arora, Karunesh Kr. and Gugnani, Vijay, 2004. Digital Library : Language Centered Research, Test Beds and Applications. International Conference on Digital Libraries. New Delhi.

14

Challenges in Library Services in Digital Era: Particular Reference to A C Joshi Library, Panjab University Chandigarh

Dr. Raj Kumar
Chief Librarian,
A.C. Joshi Library, Punjab University, Chandigarh
Neeraj Kumar Singh

INTRODUCTION

Internet and the Web have given momentum to new ways of communication and Knowledge sharing. Digital libraries are considered by many to be a key application of Internet and Web technologies. They enable the creation, organization, maintenance, management, access to, sharing and preservation of digital document collections. The current evolution in Information technology brings major changes in the way of Information communication. Information Communication technology developments opened up new avenues to e-resources publishing in a big way. E- resources is distribution of information in any electronic form such as CD- ROM, Floppy Disk or Magnetic tape or across a computer network like e-journals, E-Books, ETD etc. accessible dial-up bulletin board or on-line services

WHAT IS DIGITAL LIBRARY?

The digital library is an electronic or virtual library where information is selected, acquired, processed, organised, stored and retrieved in digital form.

ACCORDING TO WIKIPEDIA

A digital library is a library in which collections are stored in digital formats and accessible by computers.

"A digital library is an organized and focused collection of digital objects, including text, images, video and audio, along with methods for access and retrieval, and for selection, creation, organization, maintenance and sharing of the collection."

NEED OF DIGITAL LIBRARY SERVICES

The digital library services are delivered very fast as compared to the traditional method of communication. The need of the digital libraries arises due to many factors viz

i. Information explosion
ii. Resource sharing
iii. Transmission of information
iv. Information management
v. Changing needs of the users
vi. Availability of e-resources

DIGITAL LIBRARY COLLECTIONS

E-Books; E-Journals; E-Thesis and dissertation (ETD); E-News Papers; E-Reference books; CD-ROMs; Online Data bases.

E-Book

E-book is a portable hard ware and software book as a portable hardware and software system that can display a large quantity of readable textual information to the user. An e-book is commonly bundled by a publisher for distribution.

E-Journal

An e-journal is processed published and distributed all over the world by electronic network. E- Journals started with the full text databases offered by Dialog in 1980's . Linking citations and references to bibliographic database or to full- text articles make it utility more. The societies, associations, professionals' bodies and publishers like Elsevier Science, Blackwell, Wolter Kluwer, Karger, Springer, BMJ, Oxford University Press, Cambridge University Press and Nature Group etc. are providing online access to users.

E-Zine

E-Zine means electronic magazine and it is also called **web- Zine**. The articles that are stored of a file server may be distributed or accessed via a computer network. Some examples of e-zine are:

E-Newspaper

Like Electronic Theses and Dissertations, an electronic newspaper is a self contained, reusable, and refreshable version of a traditional news paper that acquires and holds all information in the news paper electronically.

CD-ROM

A compact disk- read only memory is one of a series of devices. It is use for store large amount of structured data, bibliographic information full text information and images etc. The In combination with Web server the network operating system also enable launching of CD applications from Web browsers, by clicking on hypertext links on a HTML page.

FEATURES OF E-RESOURCES

- Text can be searched, except when represented in the form of images;
- Hundreds or thousands may be carried together on one device. Approximately 500 average e-books can be stored on one CD;
- Type size and type face may be adjusted
- E-Resources can be used with text-to-speech software;
- Distributed at low cost;
- Distributed instantly, allowing readers to begin reading at once, without the need to visit a bookstore.
- No risk of damage, vandalism, etc. on the pages

Advantages of Digital Library

No physical boundary; Round the clock availability ; Multiple accesses ;Information retrieval. Preservation and conservation; Space ; Networking; Cost.

Digital Library Services

Always library services are followed by library works. But now the advancement in information technology has brought changes in the concept of traditional library work as well as service. The recent trend and change in the information related field especially in collection, storing, processing and dissemination of information have resulted in to the evolution of digital libraries .

Examples of Digital Library Services

- Access to library catalogues and union catalogues.
- Access to bibliographic databases
- Access to subject gate ways in specific disciplines
- Document delivery services
- On-line current awareness services
- Reference services provided by librarians and experts on the web

A C Joshi Library

The Panjab University Library, named officially the "A. C. Joshi Library" an illustrious Vice-Chancellor of this University, was established in the U.S. Club, Shimla in the year 1947 after the partition of the country. The foundation stone of the new Library building was laid in 1958 by Dr. S. Radhakrishnan, the then Vice-President of India. The new premises of the Library were formally inaugurated in 1963 by Pt. Jawaharlal Nehru, then the Prime Minister of India. The five-storeyed impressive library building in red stone and concrete is based on modern principles of architecture. Its modular and functional style fulfills the purpose of a planned Library. The Library building, centrally air-conditioned and equipped with computer and communication network, houses more than seven lakh volumes and has a seating capacity of 500 readers. Besides the two main reading halls there are reading rooms in the Periodicals and Special Collections Sections, and an Outer Reading Hall for studying personal books. There is a provision of 24 research carrels for teachers engaged in serious research work, and 90 lockers for research scholars. The Library has a collection of over 7 lakh publications which include books, bound volumes of journals, theses/dissertations, rare books, reports, government documents, back files of newspapers, and a prized collection of 1490 manuscripts.

E-resources @ PU Library

The book and journal collection is augmented by a variety of online sources. The Library provides access to 225 online fulltext journals as part of print journals subscription. Access to approximately 5000 online full text journals is also available through INDEST- Consortium and UGC- INFONET.

Online resources Subscribed by Panjab University Library

- Science Direct
- WESTLAW Online Database
- SCOPUS Online Citation Database
- Proquest Dissertations and Thesis Database
- Sage Online Journals
- Wiley Online Books

Access through UGC- INFONET and INDEST Consortia

- Web of Science Online Citation Database
- UGC INFONET Journals
- INDEST journals
- JCCC@UGC-INFONET E-Journal Gateway

Web of Science - It is the world's leading citation database with multidisciplinary coverage of over 10,000 high-impact journals in the sciences, social sciences, and arts and humanities, as well as international proceedings coverage for over 120,000 conferences. Powerful tools include cited reference searching, Citation Maps, and the Analyze Tool.

Science Direct - Science Direct's extensive and unique full text database covers authoritative titles from the core scientific literature, including high-impact factor titles such as THE LANCET, Cell and Tetrahedron. More than 2,500 journals and more than nine million full-text articles are available in Science Direct.

Scopus - is the largest abstract and citation database of peer-reviewed literature and quality web sources with smart tools to track, analyze and visualize research.

- Westlaw International
- Proquest Dissertations and Theses Databases
- UGC-Infonet Databases
- INDEST Databases

Digital Library Services @ PU Library

- User orientation and training: To maximize the use of library and its resources, orientation and training courses are arranged for readers. This includes helping them use the OPAC (Online Public Access Catalogue) of the library which is made available through LAN. All the departments of the university are provided with this facility. In addition to the library's stock of material, it also provides access to the library's journal holdings and theses collection.
- The users are also given training in how to use the various library online databases and the CD-ROM Network service which is also provided through LAN so that number of users are benefited at a time and they can retrieve information relevant to their needs within a reasonable time.
- Online Current Awareness Services: Online Book alert and Article alert services are provided to the faculty

members on regular basis to keep them aware about the latest resources coming in the library

- Library OPAC :
- The web OPAC of the library facilitates online catalogue search.
- There are various access points like author, title, ISBN, year, subject or call number.

Interlending and Document Delivery

Panjab University Library acts as a Document Delivery Centre for northern areas as a member of INFLIBNET and DELNET. In this, the information regarding the materials to be loaned had to be communicated or the transmission of electronic copies of the actual documents. The technological developments and the influence of internet has lead to the use of e-mail for sending and receiving requests, sending scanned copies of the material which has further enabled the reference staff to achieve high success in the faster access of information. The physical location of the materials is no longer an issue.

Challenges in Providing Digital Library Services

- Financial constraint of different institutions
- Hesitance of Staff
- Lack of necessary IT equipment and infrastructure

CONCLUSION

The recent developments in the INTERNET and in Web Technologies have brought significant changes in the concept of traditional library services. With the emergence of digital collections libraries are now providing digital library services to the users to satisfy their increasing demands through various forms of current awareness and selective dissemination of information services. Such services are provided to the users to keep them abreast of the latest developments in their field of interest through on-line search services in digital information environment. Thus the library personnel should develop their professional proficiency and communication skill in order to meet the challenges emerging out of digital library services.

15

Digital Library: Network Security Issues

Vikesh Sethi
Head, Dept. of Computer Science,
Manohar Memorial P.G. College,
Fatehabad (Haryana)

ABSTRACT

The contribution of networking technologies for a library is significant. The library network security issues are major issues for the library professionals. Libraries are changing rapidly towards digitization. Now a day's stand-alone computer is of no use. It must be on network to utilize the resources. Computer networking involves connecting desktop computers, laptops, hubs, switches and other connectivity devices. Library professional requires inside planning in providing the security to the network in respect of secured data transmission and library applications. The paper is concentrating especially on library network security.

INTRODUCTION

Digital Library systems are the computerized information storage and retrieval systems connected to the computer networks having maximum flexibility, durability, immunity, stability, scalability, accessibility and compatibility with other media at minimum cost, space and maintenance. Library network provides transmission of information dissemination of catalogues; abstract and full text formats as well as various basic functions of libraries like acquiring, digitizing and archiving of contents. The security of the network of a digital library is the major issue.

NETWORK SECURITY

The process of securing our library network begins with realizing what the library stands to lose if security is not pursued. Network security is not just "another thing to do." Its importance lies in protecting the library's network resources.

Network resource means the equipment, software and data that make up a networking system including the user data that is shared over the network. In terms of network communication, this includes the servers, workstations, hubs, switches, routers, firewalls and telecommunications links that make up a network. In terms of usage, this includes shared printers, database systems, shared software, user accounts, the shared or user-specific files stored on a central server and the keystrokes and form information that travel across the network.

IMPLEMENTING NETWORK SECURITY

I divide the realm of network security in libraries into seven main categories: physical security, password security, hardware security, server security, workstation security, perimeter security and financial security. These areas are expanded in the Checklist by separating out specific configuration issues related to web servers and general administrative issues related to budgeting, planning, and policy development.

There are many sections in the security checklist:

- General security
- Physical security of computers and network equipment
- Password security
- Hardware security
- Workstation security
- Network server security
- Network equipment security
- Switch/Router/Hub security
- Web server security

LOCAL AREA NETWORK SECURITY

Securing any computer in a library must be achieved without any compromise to these three basic concepts: public service, user privacy and legal access. In an office or business environment, security is a matter of making sure those documents and transactions haven't been tampered with, corporate information is protected, personal employee information is kept private, and data is available when the business wants it to be. Network and computer security in a library setting faces these same challenges and a few additional ones. The major local area network security points are: Password Security, Hardware Security, Workstation Security, LAN/Domain Server Security and Network Equipment Security. The librarians have to protect these levels of security in the network.

Password Security

The least expensive and most important aspect of

network security is the use of appropriate passwords. Password protection is inherent in various aspects of the network.

- Administrative access to server functions
- Workstation access to various files and services (such as the Internet)
- Administrative access to network hubs, switches, routers, and firewalls
- Access to administrative files, such as confidential personnel files or reports

Here are the checklist items related to password security:

- Develop written password policy and provide to all staff and patrons using specific user logons
- Develop written instructions in creating strong passwords and provide to all staff and patrons using specific user logons
- Document passwords for all network equipment, servers, and workstations
- Store password documentation in secure location known only by library director and one other person

Hardware Security

Hardware security is a convenient category used to classify miscellaneous items related to your computer and network hardware. The first set of items relate to the BIOS (the Basic Input Output System) of your servers and workstations. The BIOS is a well-known feature on all Intel/ AMD PC compatible servers and workstations. It performs basic tests of internal components to be sure that they are working satisfactorily. It also stores and manages the configuration of many of the parts inside the CPU case.

Workstation Security

Properly securing workstations is a very important part of the overall network security in a library. There are a large number of configuration issues to address when securing workstations. Using the Windows NT Workstation/2000 Professional operating system provides a better security foundation than does Windows XP. Those libraries using Windows XP on public workstations are highly encouraged to install special software to secure many of the workstation functions.

- Configure NT Workstation/2000 Professional partitions with NTFS file systems
- Windows NT/2000, unlike Windows XP includes a feature known as file system security

LAN/Domain Server Security

This paper assumes the use of Windows NT/2000 as the library's server operating system. In most small library local area networks, there will be one or two servers: a main server, usually a domain controller under Windows NT/2000, which verifies the logins of all users and a file server used with the library automation system. In some libraries, these two services are combined on one server. It is possible to operate in a very small environment with just Windows NT Workstation/2000 Professional-based computers and no server at all, but it is more difficult to maintain security in this environment. So this base level of security assumes the presence of at least one server. The following items are needed to secure the local area network servers in the library.

- Configure all NT Server partitions with NTFS file systems
- Configure separate operating system and data

partitions (both NTFS)

- Mirror server drives (or implement RAID), if funding allows, for redundancy
- Configure servers with private IP addresses (LAN-wide recommendation)
- Remove unnecessary services
- Remove unnecessary files/programs
- Configure file system with proper file/folder access permissions
- Restrict access to the Network Monitor Agent
- Disable anonymous user logons
- Disable caching of user logons
- Configure account policy to restrict unauthorized logon attempts
- Create logon-warning message (a warning against unauthorized logon or access and use of restricted resources)
- Create alternative Administrators group and restrict membership
- Restrict privileges of default Administrators group
- Create alternative Administrator account (with new name) with full privileges
- Disable default Administrator account
- Configure auditing of Administrator account logon attempts (to track hacking attempts)
- Set a strong password for current administrator account
- Use different passwords for domain/server accounts

than for local workstation accounts, or use different account names

- Restrict access permissions for the everyone group
- Disable Guest account if enabled
- Create appropriate user and group accounts (minimum of three groups: Patrons, Staff and Administrators)
- Set appropriate group access permissions
- Implement procedures for file backups according to backup plan
- Restrict access to backup program
- Create and maintain current Emergency Repair Disks, and store in a controlled location
- File all server component documentation (papers/ manuals/disks) for use by service technicians

Network Equipment Security

Network equipment refers to all the devices required to get data signals from one computer to another. Generally, these include hubs, switches, routers and firewalls. Libraries should be purchasing network equipment that provides management capabilities. This provides the possibility of remote management of the network even if the library does not contract for that service initially.

- Set appropriate network management protocol (SNMP) passwords/community strings
- Record and secure any password settings created by staff or contractors

These two items minimize the risk of network equipment configurations being altered by unauthorized personnel. When the library hires a vendor to install and configure network equipment, be sure to document all passwords used to secure the equipment. It is the library's responsibility to secure these passwords by documenting them and storing the documentation in a secure (preferably locked) location.

- Configure audit logs properly, if available
- Implement procedure for monitoring audit logs
- Schedule periodic installation of firmware updates
- Document equipment settings for future use in reconfiguring equipment
- File all network equipment documentation (papers/ manuals/disks) for use by service technicians.

CONCLUSION

A Library network service is a collection of digital computing, storage and communication machinery together with the software needed to reproduce, emulate and extend the services provided by the conventional libraries. The library network once established is not secured from the administrators' point of view but must provide network security policy for servers, clients and other connectivity devices to provide satisfactory level of network security.

REFERENCES

1. Joseph, J. Veda Michael, 2003. Network Administration and Security in Digital Library Environment. IN CALIBER 421-428 pp.
2. International Data Corporation, 2000. The New Ethernet URL www.intel.com/network/ethernet/ethernet_r03.pdf.
3. Data communications and Networking, Tata McGraw-Hill, New Delhi

4. Microsoft Encyclopedia of Networking, Prentice Hall of India, India.

5. www.tsl.state.tx.us

6. http://www.infopeople.org/howto/security/basics/about.html

7. Norton, Peter and Mueller, John Paul, Peter Norton's, Complete Guide to Windows NT 4 Workstation.

8. Zimmerman, Scott and Evans, Tim. Building an Intranet with Windows NT 4